KOMBUCHA
REVOLUTION

KOMBUCHA
REVOLUTION

75 Recipes for Homemade Brews, Fixers, Elixirs, and Mixers

STEPHEN LEE
FOUNDER OF KOMBUCHA WONDER DRINK
WITH KEN KOOPMAN

PHOTOGRAPHY BY LEO GONG

TEN SPEED PRESS
Berkeley

ACKNOWLEDGMENTS

There were many life-changing events for me in the 1990s, but the one that would become the beginning of this book happened in St. Petersburg, Russia. Here's to you, Mrs. Lisovski, for your inspiration, grace, and history, which propelled the launch of Kombucha Wonder Drink. You survived the Russian Revolution, several years in Siberian gulags, Stalin, wars, and thirty-five years of a declining Soviet system until Perestroika—always with your head held high, your positive attitude, and your weekly brew. Thank you, kind lady.

And to you, Ken Koopman, for your partnership, journalistic approach to research, organization, sensitivities, and creativity that have made this book possible. You and your team at Koopman Ostbo Marketing Communications are the kind of branding experts that make guys like me look good.

Thanks to my associates at Kombucha Wonder Drink for their help in the completion of this book, and to Lauren Gross for her persistent efforts that kept her in command of all the details. Lauren's can-do work ethic and positive attitude made her a joy to work with. Through this process, I met Warren Moliken, who continues to impress me as a true master of his craft. Your knowledge and expertise as a kombucha purist elevated the content on these pages to the highest level. I would also like to acknowledge my two favorite tea suppliers, Steve Smith of Steven Smith Teamaker and Veerinder Chawla of the Tao of Tea.

To Ray Colvin and all the fine people at the prestigious Oregon Culinary Institute, thank you for your tremendous help with chefs, bartenders, and all things culinary. Your class of future chefs and mixologists proved themselves to me as up-and-coming leaders in the food and beverage world.

There are so many people who lent their creativity, time, ideas, and guidance in making this project a reality. Please visit the credits at the back of this book for a listing of those who were involved.

Thanks to Lisa Westmoreland and the team at Ten Speed Press for recognizing kombucha as a category worthy of publishing a book. I feel privileged to be joining them in spreading the word about the wonder of kombucha.

Another person who deserves special thanks for promoting all things kombucha is Hannah Crum, known as "Kombucha Mamma" to thousands of kombucha enthusiasts all over the world. Her industry leadership and generous sharing of information on her Kombucha Kamp website have given a tremendous boost to home brewers and manufacturers alike.

Much appreciation and applause goes to the dozens of my fellow kombucha entrepreneurs who have joined the mystical brewing bandwagon over the past ten years. I salute you! Finally, I would like to acknowledge the rich, millennium-long fermenting history of kombucha and the first person who discovered a SCOBY on top of some tea that had been left outside his hut for several days and decided it was a worthy drink to consume and share with friends.

To Mrs. Lisovski

INTRODUCTION

Kombucha. It's been called the "elixir of life," a cure-all that detoxifies the body, aids digestion, reenergizes the mind, and even helps reverse the symptoms of cancer. Drink several glasses of this fermented tea a day and, according to some, its healing properties will lower cholesterol, help with weight loss, reduce hot flashes, and create a general sense of well-being.

Its origins are shrouded in mystery. Two-thousand-year-old fables tell of exhausted warriors rejuvenating their weary bodies by drinking a fermented concoction infused with tea leaves. Even its name, pronounced com-BOO-cha, connotes something both alien and ancient. Nobody seems to know where it came from or how long it's been around.

I discovered kombucha on one of my many tea-selling trips to Russia. I had been in the tea business for more than twenty years at the time, and while I had heard about this exotic tea drink called kombucha, I had never tasted it. One night I was having dinner with an associate at his St. Petersburg apartment. Peter lived with his mother—I knew her only as Mrs. Lisovski—and after a wonderful meal of borscht, piroshkies, and lots of pickled vegetables, I excused myself to use their loo. On my way down the narrow hall, I looked through an open door on my right and saw something strange.

There, on the nightstand next to Mrs. Lisovski's bed, was a one-gallon jug of brownish liquid with cheesecloth stretched over the top. I felt ridiculously guilty peering into the bedroom of an eighty-year-old woman, but I couldn't resist taking a closer look at that jar. Straining my eyes in the dim light, I saw something really odd. There was a pancake-sized gelatinous blob floating on top of the fluid.

When I returned to the kitchen, I admitted to Peter that I had looked into his mother's bedroom, and then rather sheepishly asked what was in the glass jar. He laughed and then reached into the refrigerator. He pulled out a pitcher and poured us both a glass. "It's kombucha. My mother calls it mushroom tea," he told me.

When I tasted Mrs. Lisovski's brew, I was amazed. There was effervescence to it—the lightly carbonated beverage tickled my tongue—with a tanginess that my taste buds told me was like an apple cider flavor. The finish was slightly acidic, yet the overall mouth feel was very pleasurable. I had never experienced anything like it.

I begged for the story behind this wonderful drink. Through Peter's translation, Mrs. Lisovski related the story of how her great aunt from Siberia had passed down the recipe for her *chainii grib*. She received her "mother" culture in 1939 and had been making a batch every week since. I later did the math and marveled at the fact I was drinking batch number 2,860 of Mrs. Lisovski's personal brew. What blew me away was before I left the apartment, the lovely little lady presented me with a peeled-off section of this grayish-white patty (think bottom half of a hamburger bun). I knew what it was (after all, I had spied it on her nightstand), but I didn't know what I was supposed to do with it. Peter explained that it was common practice for anyone who made "mushroom tea" to peel off the top layer of the "mother" and give it to a neighbor or friend so they could use it to make their own batch of kombucha.

Carrying on the Legacy

Mrs. Lisovski's gift changed my life. On those three long plane rides home from St. Petersburg, Russia, to Portland, Oregon, I stayed awake thinking about all the different ways I could incorporate kombucha into my life. One couldn't get away with it today, but fortunately for me, three kind stewardesses stored Mrs. Lisovski's "mother" culture and some tea in a jar in their galley refrigerators. The precious cargo made it safely to my pantry where I began home brewing my own kombucha. I'm proud to say that for many years I carried on the legacy of Mrs. Lisovski's Siberian aunt, extending her unbroken streak of using her "mother" culture to brew a new batch of kombucha every week for more than 3,000 weeks.

I never really considered myself a master brewer of kombucha, but I got pretty good at it. I enjoyed making kombucha so much I decided to dedicate the next phase of my business life to brewing and selling kombucha on a large scale. As I had done when we built Stash Tea and later Tazo Tea (which sold to Starbucks), I assembled a team of experts to help me create a commercial manufacturing company, which we called Kombucha Wonder Drink. We went to market with three flavors—traditional, lemon, and Asian pear ginger. Some of my fondest memories are of experimenting with the different flavors one can infuse with kombucha.

What Is Kombucha?

Kombucha is a fermented beverage made with brewed tea, sugar, and bacteria that is introduced from a starter culture. Depending on the amount of sugar used, fermentation time, and temperature, the flavor of any one kombucha can range from tart to sour to tangy. Large-scale manufacturers as well as home brewers blend kombucha with herbs, fruit, spices, infused teas, and other flavors to create their own concoctions.

The key to kombucha's existence is the *mother*, a live starter culture similar to a sourdough bread starter. Referred to in the industry as a SCOBY (Symbiotic Colony of Bacteria and Yeast), this rubbery substance kicks off the fermentation process and ultimately forms a pancake-size disk that looks like the top of a mushroom (thus, the reason why for centuries the drink was called "mushroom tea"). Historically, fermentation has been celebrated for creating alcoholic beverages like mead, beer, and wine, but it is also valued for its usefulness in

Stephen Lee (right) joins Head Brewer David Treece (left) in the fermentation room for a quality-control test of a recently brewed batch of Kombucha Wonder Drink's raw kombucha.

preserving foods (who can forget Grandma's pickled cucumbers?). For the purposes of this book, fermentation can be defined as the transformation of food by various bacteria, fungi, and the enzymes they produce. This process involves anaerobic metabolism, the production of energy from nutrients without oxygen. (For more about fermentation, I recommend reading Sandor Katz's *The Art of Fermentation*.) Regarding the question "Is there alcohol in kombucha?" home brewers can expect an alcohol content of below 0.5 percent. Commercially sold kombucha brewed to create an alcohol content higher than 0.5 percent may only be purchased by those twenty-one years and older.

Kombucha is alive, teeming with beneficial microorganisms and active bacterial cultures that, much like the live cultures in yogurt, provide the body with a great source of nutrition. With its probiotic properties that help balance the "good" and "bad" bacteria in the intestinal tract, kombucha is regarded by many as a "wonder" food as opposed to just a healthy drink. But even though this magical tonic has been around for centuries and is chock-full of probiotics, B vitamins, and amino acids, its purported health benefits remain unproven.

Brief History of Kombucha

The ancient Chinese referred to it as "the tea of immortality," so, who knows, maybe kombucha has been around forever. No one knows for sure. The research I've done has led me to believe people were brewing the bubbly fermented beverage thousands of years ago in huts and villages in Asia and Eastern Europe. Stories have been passed down through the ages that Genghis Khan and his traveling armies carried a fermented, vinegary beverage in their wineskins to give them strength and stamina on long marches.

In my travels to tea meccas like Japan, China, and India, I had heard passing references to a mysterious fermented tea—the Japanese called it *kocha kinoko* (red tea mushroom) and the Chinese, *hongchajun* (red tea fungus).

And where did the name come from? A little too convenient perhaps, but another story has a Korean doctor named Dr. Kombu delivering it to Japanese Emperor Inyoko in 414 AD *Gribok*, as the Russians affectionately called their "little mushroom" beverage, was supposed to have saved Nobel Prize–winner Aleksandr Solzhenitsyn's life when he was in exile in Siberia. More recently, there's the tale told about the Russians who lived through the Chernobyl nuclear meltdown in the late 1980s; a common thread among those who survived the radiation exposure was that they regularly consumed kombucha.

The Popularity of Kombucha Today

In America, those who grew up in the 1960s and 1970s may remember people experimenting with home-brewed "hippie tea." Today, those recipes from the back-to-nature era have been resurrected, and brewing kombucha at home has become a popular cottage industry.

When I started Kombucha Wonder Drink in 2001, there were not many of us manufacturing kombucha on a large scale. Today, there are several with national distribution into mainstream grocery stores and more than a hundred mostly small to medium-size regional companies making and bottling a commercial kombucha drink. In the most current data, natural products industry experts reported sales of kombucha products at more than $370 million. With the growth I'm seeing, $500 million in sales is right around the corner.

Visit any college campus in America, and you'll see that sugary soda drinks are on the decline, and healthy functional beverages—vitamin waters, enhanced fruit drinks, and so on—are on the rise. Celebrities are pictured in magazines drinking kombucha. Medical experts are holding up bottles of kombucha on their TV shows and advising people to switch from high-fructose drinks.

DAILY KOMBUCHA

Whether you brew your own kombucha or buy it from a store, I would recommend incorporating it into your diet by drinking 4 to 8 ounces of kombucha two times a day. It's a good idea to drink plenty of water in addition to the kombucha to help flush out any toxins in your body and space out your consumption so your system has more time to absorb the vitamins and amino acids. Since my body has acclimated to the natural restorative properties of kombucha, I sometimes consume more, adding a third portion in the evening. Just remember, everything in moderation.

When people ask me when is the best time of day to drink kombucha, I tell them any time is great. I like to start my day with a kombucha smoothie or blended with some juice. I call it my Fixer because it sets my body in motion and gives me energy. Usually after lunch I'll pop open a bottle of what I call my Elixir—Kombucha Wonder Drink's Essence of Juniper Berry, Spearmint & Lemon Myrtle, or another favorite of my mine, Kombucha Wonder Drink's Asian Pear & Ginger Kombucha. In the evening, I like to relax with a drink I make with my Traditional Kombucha Wonder Drink and a few drops of bitters. Sometimes I add an ounce of Aviation American Gin or Crater Lake Vodka, both from local distilleries here in Oregon. I call this my Mixer.

In my Portland neighborhood alone, there are at least a dozen places where I can go and have my choice of several kombucha beverages on tap. My prediction is that soon most neighborhoods in America will feature several establishments that serve kombucha. And even if you don't know where to buy it, you can always make your own.

For centuries, perhaps millennia, the "boil, steep, ferment" approach to brewing kombucha has worked just fine. Its ease is what has made kombucha so approachable for do-it-yourselfers. It's still a simple process, but there's so much more you can do to make it your own special brew. The artisanal culinary movement has breathed new life into how we approach so many old-world favorites: wine, coffee, ice cream, chocolate, and pickles. Time to put kombucha at the top of that list.

In doing my research for this book, I've met dozens of talented brewers who've inspired me with their creative skills and culinary craftsmanship. And I've learned there is an emerging community of sophisticated kombucha makers who are finding new ways to improve on an old-world craft.

Your Kombucha Kit

Before you start home-brewing your own kombucha in chapter 1, you'll need to gather some key ingredients, equipment, and know-how.

It All Starts with the Tea

All tea comes from the *Camellia sinensis* plant. From this one plant, six distinct families of tea are produced: black, green, white, yellow, oolong, and pu-erh. Tea has more than 2,000 years of rich cultural tradition and experimentation that has produced the different styles of tea, and the taste of each harvest is affected by the age of the plant, its elevation, the richness of the soil, and the climatic conditions during that season. Right now we're living in a real tea renaissance, where great teas are abundant, affordable, and accessible. Before starting the kombucha-brewing process, I recommend you brew yourself a cup of the tea you're considering using in an infusion or recipe and see how you like it. If it tastes good to you, I can pretty much guarantee you'll like the taste of the (plain) kombucha made from it.

When deciding which tea to use for your infusion or recipe, a general rule of thumb is black tea kombuchas are usually stronger brews. With its bolder acid notes, a black tea will compete more aggressively with an infused flavor and can overwhelm delicate fruit pairings. An oolong or green tea kombucha will better suit an infusion. If properly brewed (as in not overfermented), the tart and fermented oolong and green tea kombucha character will be more delicate and allow subtle citrus or pomegranate notes to shine through. But feel free to experiment. It's your creation. Just as the vintner who oversees his crop from flower to fruit to barrel to bottle but doesn't know if the vintage will be memorable, you won't know if your kombucha will be tasty until you taste the final result.

What's a SCOBY?

There would be no such thing as kombucha without the SCOBY. So, it is the most critical component of the brewing process. To start, you'll need to source your SCOBY online, at a homesteading store, or from a friend. (Note: While it's possible to grow your own SCOBY from a mixture of kombucha, water, tea, and sugar, whenever sugars are thriving in an environment without a SCOBY, the possibility of undesirable bacteria becoming dominant is much greater, so we don't recommend it.)

SCOBY is short for Symbiotic Colony of Bacteria and Yeast. It's what ferments your tea. Historically, this bacteria and yeast complex has been called "the mother" because it will reproduce itself every time you brew a new batch. From the moment the original SCOBY is delicately laid upon the surface of the sweetened tea, she begins to grow another SCOBY. This new culture (called the baby) always grows on top of the original, at the liquid-air interface. It begins as a barely detectable translucent film and eventually thickens and turns pale beige. It has two distinct sides—the lower side often has brown yeast strands growing from it and prefers contact with the liquid, while the upper layer needs contact with the air and will eventually appear and feel dry.

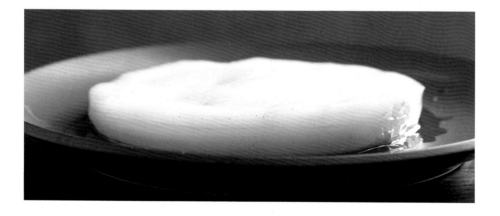

Indeed, the SCOBY is slimy to the touch. Its rubbery texture comes from its cellulose structure, which provides a home for the beneficial microscopic colonies.

If you're brewing a new batch at the time you're harvesting the finished kombucha, you can continue to use the same fused mother/baby SCOBY in the new batch. Alternatively, you can separate them and pass one on to a friend. This is how I got started (thanks again, Mrs. Lisovski!) and this is the sharing "culture" of kombucha-brewing enthusiasts.

A SCOBY-Friendly Environment

Be aware that SCOBYs prefer glass. A metal vessel can leach harmful elements that will weaken a SCOBY. Food-grade plastic can be used, but brewers usually work with glass or nonleaded ceramic. Also make sure to rinse your hands often with water and dry your hands with a clean towel. You don't want soaps, detergents, lotions, or antibacterial agents coming into contact with the SCOBY.

Putting Your SCOBY to Rest

If you don't flow directly from one batch into another, be sure to put your SCOBY to rest properly. This means that it has sweetened tea (use 4 cups purified water, $1/4$ cup evaporated cane sugar, and 4 to 6 bags tea) for sustenance, remains covered, and doesn't get too cold (the SCOBY requires a temperature range as close to 68°F to 72°F as possible). If things get too cold, the yeast and bacteria go dormant, and undesirable bacteria have a good chance to colonize. Even worse, this situation could cause mold growth—green or black spore colonies, just like the mold that grows on bread. If this happens, throw your SCOBY away and get a new one. If the weeks when you don't brew drag on, just add more sweetened tea, removing and discarding some of the fermented tea about once a month. When you're ready to begin again, rinse the SCOBY in cool water to remove the yeast strands. You could separate the kombucha mother from the baby that has grown and use both to get two brews going. Or you could pass the older mother to a friend. Compost heaps and chickens also love SCOBYs. When SCOBYs rest, the baby grows quite thick and has a tendency to adhere firmly to the mother. You may have a situation where you need to tear one part from the other. There is nothing wrong with using the entire SCOBY in your next batch or tearing off a portion of it if it becomes too unwieldy.

Important: If you find any mold on your SCOBY, throw it away along with the kombucha and start over.

BOOCHIE SALT SCRUB

Esthetician Oona Johanna Meade's "light bulb" business idea happened one night as she was reaching in her refrigerator for a bottle of kombucha. The light bulb in the fridge hadn't been working, but as she was thinking, "If I am putting this in my body for the antiaging, antioxidizing properties, why not put it *on* my largest organ . . . my skin," the light bulb magically came on. She took that as a sign to develop a skincare product so pure you could eat it. The result was Komboona Skincare, which uses dried SCOBYs in tonics and products such as this salt scrub. It's a great way to reuse your SCOBY to detoxify, cleanse, and soften rough, calloused skin. Lemongrass is known to promote circulation, and breathing in its essential oils offers relaxation as well as clarity.

1 SCOBY (see page 7)

4 cups coarse-grind Himalayan pink salt

1 tablespoon lemongrass essential oil

2 tablespoons plain kombucha (page 19)

With each batch of home-brewed kombucha, a new layer will form on the SCOBY. This new layer can be easily peeled away and used separately. When a SCOBY is ready to separate from the mother, take the "baby" and dry it overnight by suspending it from a clothesline with clothespins. After it has dried, place it in a clean coffee grinder, and grind it until it is a coarse grind.

Place 4 cups of Himalayan salt in a mixing bowl, add the ground SCOBY, toss with your hands. Add 1 tablespoon lemongrass essential oil and stir it with a spatula. Add in the kombucha a few drops at a time, stirring the entire time. The scrub will be moist and coarse.

Set yourself up with some towels and a galvanized wash tub. Pour in some boiled water that is warm enough for a foot bath. Get comfy, place your feet in the wash tub, grab a handful of Boochie Salt Scrub, and scrub the bottom of your feet, in between your toes and up onto your calves. Enjoy the detoxifying and healing experience of the concoction.

When you are finished with the scrub, pour warm water over your legs and feet to cleanse them as well as activate the lemongrass, which offers you an aromatherapeutic foot bath finish to your kombucha foot scrub. A divine way to end a long day on your feet!

Starter Tea

Starter tea is previously brewed kombucha or store-bought raw kombucha with no flavorings or infusions (essentially as close as possible to a traditional plain kombucha). It is added to freshly brewed sweetened tea to lower the pH and introduce a plethora of beneficial yeasts and bacteria to help kick-start the fermentation process.

Purified Water

The recipes in this book call for purified water. Water quality is very important. If your local municipal system adds chlorine or fluoride, it's necessary to remove the chlorine. You don't need a filter, just leave your pot of tap water on the counter for 24 hours to allow the chlorine to evaporate. Caution: boiling water for a long time can cause loss of dissolved oxygen, which leads to flat-tasting water (this critical mistake most often accounts for poor-tasting tea).

Evaporated Cane Sugar

Sugar plays an important role: it's food for your SCOBY! The fermentation process is driven by the bacteria and yeast thriving on the sugars. If you can, avoid the white processed stuff and use organic, evaporated, Fair Trade cane sugar. It is slightly less processed than white sugar and will yield a nice amber tone in your final brew. By choosing Fair Trade, you are showing respect for an industry and its workers.

Thermometer

A basic kitchen thermometer, such as an instant-read, is not required but highly recommended, because each variety of tea requires a different steeping temperature. At under $20, this could be the single biggest factor in creating your best kombucha.

Cotton Cloth

A clean cotton cloth enables breathability for the bacteria and yeast living within the SCOBY to do their jobs. The cloth cover also acts to keep out dust, fruit flies, gnats, and other flying critters, but does not exclude the oxygen needed for the bacteria and yeast living in the SCOBY. Do not use cheesecloth, which is porous enough to allow fruit fly eggs to fall through the weave.

You can also use an old cotton T-shirt—just make sure it's clean! You can use a rubber band to hold it in place around the jar.

Brewing Jar

In every situation, the wider the brewing jar the better. That's because a wider container provides a larger area at the liquid-air interface (the surface of the liquid). During fermentation, the new SCOBY will grow at the surface and fully occupy the inner dimensions of your vessel. The larger the jar, the bigger the SCOBY. And a bigger SCOBY means a faster fermentation process, and the sooner you'll be enjoying your freshly brewed kombucha. A SCOBY is basically a floating sugar-eating machine. The larger the area at its underside where the bacteria and yeast meet the sweetened tea, the quicker and more efficiently the sugars will be consumed during fermentation.

Practically speaking, your hand should be able to fit inside the jar. You will need to place and remove your SCOBY when putting up a new batch and during bottling. Hence, small-mouth and "tapered-at-the-top" jars present problems. Available at most stores where canning gear is sold are 1-gallon storage jars from Anchor Hocking (they have a glass lid that you'll swap out for your breathable cloth cover). This size will work well with the recipes contained herein. Otherwise, you can also use two half-gallon Ball brand mason jars.

Bottles

All glass bottles are not created equal, so choose yours carefully. If a glass bottle is not manufactured to withstand pressure, you could have an explosion on your hands, especially during the (optional) secondary fermentation stage where capped bottles will have pressure building inside. If you want to safely recycle, use any bottle with a screw cap that originally held a carbonated beverage. Alternately, any home-brew shop supplying DIY beer and wine enthusiasts will have pressure-capable bottles. The flip-top bottle (Grolsch-type) is my favorite type because it is reusable and it keeps a very tight seal. Some brewers prefer plastic bottles because they can feel the bottle to tell if a good deal of pressure from carbonation has built up, which means it's time to refrigerate.

The recipes in this cookbook call for eight to ten 16-ounce bottles. Why this variance? During the brewing process, the tea leaf absorbs a certain amount of water. During the fermentation period, some tea is lost to evaporation. Fill levels will be different depending on the shape of the bottles you're using. With these variables in mind and a starting recipe that calls for a gallon of liquid, your final

harvest of fermented kombucha will always be a bit different. Expect a yield of eight to ten bottles. Remember, you are craft-brewing using a living culture. This is not an exact science; there are many variables that can have an effect on your final volume of kombucha in the bottle.

Additional Brewing Equipment

As shown in the photo, you'll also need a few other items to complete your brewing kit: a colander or mesh strainer, measuring cups, a slotted spoon, a timer, a plastic funnel, and a fine-mesh strainer. You'll also need a 6- to 8-quart stainless steel pot and lid for steeping tea, plus an additional stockpot or vessel to decant your steeped tea.

Note: It is a good practice to start by scrubbing your brewing equipment with a new, and thus clean, scouring pad, warm water, and soap. Give everything a good rinse to remove all soap residues.

MEASUREMENTS AND SCALING

Do you measure or weigh your ingredients?

Most recipes call for volume measure. This means the sugar and tea measures are in quarts, cups, or teaspoons. This system is also called the Imperial System. Other recipes may list ingredients by weight, which requires a kitchen scale. Weighing tea and sugar makes your kombucha-brewing life much easier; metric measures allow for greater precision. Metrics also make scaling your kombucha recipes (making larger batches) easier to calculate.

Here are two identical ingredient amounts for a batch of kombucha, one using Imperial measures, one using metric measures. Either can be scaled up for any size batch:

IMPERIAL MEASURES	METRIC MEASURES
4 cups purified water	1 liter water
6 to 7 teaspoons loose-leaf tea	10 to 12 grams loose-leaf tea
1/4 cup evaporated cane sugar	50 grams evaporated cane sugar
1/2 cup starter tea	100 milliliters starter tea

Whichever method you choose (stick to one method throughout), measure out your water in a pot and set on the stove to heat. Tea and sugar are measured and set aside.

Chapter 1

HOME BREWS AND INFUSIONS

My personal roots are deeply embedded in the world of tea. Even my fortuitous discovery of kombucha happened on one of my many tea adventures. Kombucha is brewed tea, albeit a cultured version. But it's mostly water, tea, the kombucha culture, and some sugars left after the fermentation process is complete. Respect for the quality of ingredients and the reverence with which you treat them will help you make a kombucha wonder drink that will make you proud. In this section, you will also find several of my favorite flavors to infuse into your kombucha, including pomegranate, lavender, citrus, and ginger. There's no hard-and-fast rule as to when to add the ingredients for your infusions—some choose to infuse at the initial tea-brewing stage, others at the boiling stage. Have fun sharing your creations with friends!

10 BREWING TIPS FROM KOMBUCHA WONDER DRINK'S
BREW MASTER WARREN MOLIKEN

Kombucha is a living drink. There is an energy that goes into its creation that some believe can have an effect on the vitality of the final brew. For many, brewing becomes a meditative practice. When you are ready to start a new batch:

1. Practice the five Ps: Prior Preparation Prevents Poor Performance (get your stuff together and measure the ingredients).

2. Pick a brewing place—such as a tidy workspace in a clean kitchen—where you feel comfortable. This also pays off when it's time to clean up.

3. Have a dedicated kombucha-brewing notebook by your side. This will keep you organized and can serve as a checklist for each batch you make.

4. Play your favorite music. Focus, smile, breathe. Put the frenetic pace of the day's multitasking activities behind you and relax. You're about to create magic.

5. Know your SCOBY. Be gentle when handling it. Always rinse it with cool clean water. At the bottling stage, carefully rest it on a porcelain or glass plate or bowl bathed in kombucha.

6. To imbue more delicate flavors into your kombucha, use loose-leaf, higher-end teas.

7. Brew with care; don't just toss a tea bag into a pot of boiling water.

8. Use a thermometer and never overboil your water.

9. User a timer and never oversteep your leaf.

10. If brewing multiple flavors of kombucha, segregate your SCOBYs by tea type, as over time they take on the flavor profiles of the green, black, or oolong teas you use.

STEPHEN LEE'S MASTER PLAIN KOMBUCHA RECIPE

I learned how to brew kombucha through experimentation, and I highly recommend you do the same. Using different teas, such as black, green, or oolong, will produce subtlely different flavors of kombucha. Other variables include water temperature, steeping time, as well as time and temperature for the fermentation process. When you're ready to start, remember to be kind to yourself—your first few batches of home brewed kombucha may taste different than the commercially available brands. Just like with commercially produced beer and wine, commercially produced kombucha involves trained fermentation specialists who practice their skills daily and have developed methods to manufacture a consistent product. Don't be surprised if your first few batches have variable flavor profiles. Keep on trying and you will be richly rewarded with a kombucha you and your friends will fall in love with. MAKES 1 GALLON

EQUIPMENT

1-gallon glass jar or
2 half-gallon jars

6- to 8-quart stainless steel
pot and lid (for steeping tea)

Additional stockpot or vessel
to decant steeped tea

Colander or mesh strainer

Measuring cups

Slotted spoon

Timer

Thermometer

Clean cotton cloth

Rubber bands

Straw

Plastic funnel

Fine-mesh strainer

8 to 10 (16-ounce) sealable
bottles, preferably glass,
either screw-top or flip-top

Heat 6 cups of the water to 212°F for black tea, 170°F for green tea, 185°F for oolong over medium heat in a 6- to 8-quart stainless steel pot.

Remove the water from the heat and add the tea. Stir well and cover the pot with the lid to keep the steeping temperature consistent, which ensures the best flavor extraction. Steep for 4 minutes for black and green tea; steep for 5 minutes for oolong. Stir once midway through the steeping period.

If you have steeped with tea bags, use a spoon or tongs to remove the bags. If you have used loose-leaf tea, pour the tea through a colander or fine mesh strainer into second pot (see lefthand photo, page 20). Compost the tea leaves.

continued

INGREDIENTS

14 cups purified water
(see page 10)

16 to 20 tea bags; or
8 tablespoons (35 grams)
loose-leaf black tea
or green tea, 6 tablespoons
(35 grams) balled oolong
tea, or 10 tablespoons
(35 grams) loose open-leaf
oolong tea

1 cup evaporated cane
sugar (see page 10)

2 cups starter tea
(see page 10)

1 or 2 SCOBYs (Symbiotic
Colony of Bacteria and
Yeast, see page 7) (1 per
fermentation jar)

Add the sugar to the brewed tea and stir until dissolved. Add the remaining 8 cups of water. Stir. This trick reduces the temperature quickly. Be sure the tea has cooled to room temperature (72°F or cooler), as adding a live kombucha culture to water hotter than 72°F can harm the culture.

Add the starter tea and stir. Pour the entire batch of kombucha tea into the 1-gallon jar or divide it between two smaller jars.

With rinsed hands, carefully lay your SCOBY on the surface of the tea (see righthand photo, below). To divide a first-use SCOBY between two jars, separate by layers if you can, peeling them apart into two thinner round SCOBYs. If your original SCOBY is fused so that you cannot separate by layer, simply cut the SCOBY in half into two half circles with a sharp knife. It should float at the surface at least 1 inch below the rim of your jar to create enough breathing room that the SCOBY doesn't touch the cover. If there is too much tea, draw some off with a small cup and discard. If the SCOBY sinks, don't fret. All will be fine.

Cover the opening of the jar(s) with a clean cotton cloth and hold it in place with a rubber band (see photo, page 18).

Place your jar in a warm spot (72°F to 78°F) and leave your kombucha undisturbed to ferment for 7 days. A closet or closed room works best. Do not store in direct sunlight.

After a week, taste your kombucha. The easiest way to get a taste without greatly disturbing the SCOBY is to slip a straw down the inside of the jar between the glass and the edge of the SCOBY (see lefthand photo, below). Have a sip. Does it taste too sweet? Let it go a few more days before tasting again. Is it sufficiently tart and you love it? Great! Time for the next step.

Carefully remove the SCOBY with rinsed hands. You will now have the original and the new baby, which has grown on top of the mother culture. Place them on a clean porcelain or glass plate or bowl (see righthand photo, below) bathed in kombucha. They will be the cultures for your next batch, which you can either start right away, or you can put your SCOBY to rest for a while (see page 8). If you wish, you can gently rinse the SCOBY under cool water to remove any yeast strands.

Reserve about 2 cups of the finished kombucha for the starter tea for your next brew. You can use this starter tea immediately if you are starting your next brew or you can store it in the refrigerator for up to 10 days, bringing it to room temperature before its next use. (Keep in mind that a strong starter tea can affect the flavor of your next batch of kombucha.)

continued

Now you're ready to bottle. Fill your bottles with the kombucha tea using a spouted measuring cup (for an easy pour) and a plastic funnel, leaving about 1 inch of air space in the neck of the bottle. Some brewers prefer to use a fine-mesh strainer as they bottle to filter out yeast strands and small particles of tea. (See lefthand photo, below. Note: Yeast strands should be discarded; however, yeast strands and the sediment at the bottom of your fermentation jar is a great source for the yeast called for in the Harvest Breakfast Bread recipe, page 120.) Cap tightly. If you prefer a flat kombucha—drinkable, but not crisp and dry like bubbly kombucha—then refrigerate immediately after brewing, and the fermentation process will cease (no more bubbles).

For those who prefer a bubbly kombucha beverage, you will want to proceed with the secondary fermentation process. Instead of refrigerating your recently brewed kombucha, set the capped bottles aside in a warm, dark, undisturbed spot. A general rule of thumb is to store the bottles in a place where the temperature ranges between 72°F to 78°F. Note that the fermentation process will accelerate at higher temperatures. The critical piece is knowing how long to allow your bottled kombucha to continue fermenting before stopping the process through refrigeration. This is dependent on many factors—many of which are out of your control, such as the amount of sugars left at the bottling step or the type of tannins in the original tea. This is where your ongoing experience plays a part, and it helps to take good notes to refer back to what did and what did not work.

If you like your kombucha on the less sweet side, leave the bottles in the secondary fermentation process a bit longer, because the longer the fermentation process, the more sugar is "eaten." Usually, wait 48 hours, and then pop one in the refrigerator to chill for at least 6 hours. (A warm bottle will always be too bubbly and often explosive.) Crack it open. Pour into a glass. If it effervesces, you've done it! (See righthand photo, opposite page.) Chill the remaining bottles to stop the secondary fermentation process. If you want more carbonation, let it go for a few more days and test again with another chilled bottle.

Creating a bubbly kombucha is one of the trickiest steps in the process. If it takes a few batches to get it right, consider this your "on-the-job" training to become a home brewing expert. Remember, kombucha without bubbles has the same health-promoting properties as champagne-like kombucha.

Kombucha generally has a long shelf life due to its naturally protective low pH. In fact, I know of brewers who have stored their raw kombucha for years, drank it, and it was fine. I would advise storing raw home brew under refrigeration, as continued fermentation in the bottle without refrigeration can result in an exploding bottle, if the bottle is not made of pressure-capable glass.

HARVESTING YOUR KOMBUCHA

Perhaps the biggest challenge for those new to kombucha brewing is deciding when to harvest (or bottle). Sure, we bottle our kombucha when it's ready. But I've always viewed this critical stage as much more like a harvest. We've chosen select ingredients to craft our own kombucha. We've created this restorative tincture using an ancient fermentation process. We've tasted it along the way to capture it at peak flavor. It's a living food that took time to grow and mature. We're reserving some of our precious harvest to enable production of a future batch. If the kombucha will go through a secondary fermentation, we've got to exercise more patience before our bounty is to be enjoyed. And if we're simultaneously brewing another batch, we'll be sowing the seeds for next week's harvest. Yes, kombucha harvest is the part when we bottle, but then again it's so much more.

I like to tell people your finished kombucha tea is ready to drink when it has a balance of sour tartness and still detectable sweetness. In a perfect world, you are seeking a flavor that *you* enjoy. Of course, this is a highly personal preference. Some diehards love a strong, super-sour kombucha, allowing the SCOBY to work its magic for 14 (or more) days. Others prefer a gentle kombucha and bottle on the younger side (6 days). Sometimes people forget about their kombucha brew, and when they rediscover it, it has overfermented. You can tell that a batch has overfermented because it has become highly acidic and unpalatable. Not a worry, as this can be used in a salad dressing in place of vinegar (see Kombucha Vinegar recipe on page 96).

CITRUS KOMBUCHA

Get your dose of vitamin C in a variety of ways by choosing which citrus fruits you want to infuse in this drink. I'm partial to limes, but feel free to substitute tangerines, oranges, grapefruits, or lemons—or a blend! Citrus juice can vary from sweet and tart to extremely sour, so you'll want to experiment with how much to add. Citrus has well-pronounced flavors, so you won't need much. Just be sure to avoid including any of the white inner portion of the peel, known as the pith, because it is generally bitter to the taste.

MAKES 1 GALLON

14 cups purified water

16 to 20 tea bags or 8 tablespoons (35 grams) loose-leaf black tea

1 cup evaporated cane sugar

2 cups starter tea (see page 10)

1 SCOBY (see page 7)

³/₄ cup freshly squeezed lime juice (about 6 limes)

Heat 6 cups of the water in a stainless steel saucepan to 212°F, then remove from the heat. Add the tea, stir well, and cover. Steep for 4 minutes, stirring once at 2 minutes. Remove the tea bags or pour the tea through a colander or fine-mesh strainer into a second pot. Compost the tea.

Add the sugar and stir until dissolved. Then add the remaining 8 cups of water to cool the tea to about room temperature (72°F or cooler). Add the starter tea and stir. Pour into a 1-gallon jar.

With rinsed hands, carefully lay your SCOBY on the surface of the tea. Cover the opening of the jar with a clean cotton cloth and hold it in place with a rubber band. Place your jar in a warm spot (72°F to 78°F) out of direct sunlight and leave your kombucha undisturbed to ferment for 7 days.

Taste the kombucha, using a straw. Does it taste too sweet? Let it go a few more days before tasting again. Is it sufficiently tart and you love it? Great! Time for the next step.

Carefully remove the SCOBY with rinsed hands and place on a clean porcelain or glass plate or bowl bathed in kombucha. This will be your culture for the next batch.

If immediately proceeding with another batch, reserve about 2 cups of the finished kombucha for the starter tea of your next brew. (Otherwise, to put your SCOBY to rest, see page 8.)

Time to incorporate your flavoring. Using a funnel, divide the lime juice equally among the bottles (about 1½ tablespoons per 16-ounce bottle).

Top off the bottles with the harvested kombucha, leaving 1 inch of air space in the neck of the bottle. As you pour, you may want to use a fine-mesh strainer to filter out yeast strands. Cap tightly.

To begin the optional secondary fermentation, simply store the capped bottles in a warm dry place (72°F to 82°F is best) for 48 hours. Be aware that the sugars present will add fuel to the fermentation action in the bottle, which will increase the pressure inside the bottles. After 48 hours, chill one of the bottles for at least 6 hours. Crack it open and pour into a glass. If it effervesces, you've done it! If you want more carbonation, let it go for a few more days and test again with another chilled bottle. When you're pleased with the carbonation, refrigerate all the bottles to end the fermentation.

GINGER KOMBUCHA

It's one of the funniest-looking roots you'll ever come across, with its knobby appendages and gnarly brown skin, but ginger root offers a distinct and unforgettable flavor—hot, spicy, pungent, aromatic. It's one of my all-time favorite spices because it can enhance everything from stir-fries to desserts to my favorite drink—kombucha. I always keep fresh ginger root in my kitchen because I never know when I will want to grate, slice, or peel some of its fibrous flesh to "kick it up a notch" for whatever meal I'm preparing. Fresh ginger root is available year-round and keeps well in the refrigerator—generally up to 3 weeks if left unpeeled. MAKES 1 GALLON

14 cups purified water

16 to 20 tea bags or 8 tablespoons (35 grams) loose-leaf black tea

1 cup evaporated cane sugar

2 cups starter tea (see page 10)

1 SCOBY (see page 7)

2- to 4-inch knob fresh ginger root, sliced small enough to fit in the bottles (do not peel)

Heat 6 cups of the water in a stainless steel saucepan to 212°F, then remove from heat. Add the tea, stir well, cover, and steep for 4 minutes, stirring once at 2 minutes. Remove the tea bags or pour tea through a colander or fine-mesh strainer into a second pot. Compost the tea.

Add the sugar and stir until dissolved. Then add the remaining 8 cups of water to cool the tea to about room temperature (72°F or cooler). Add the starter tea and stir. Pour into a 1-gallon jar.

With rinsed hands, carefully lay your SCOBY on the surface of the tea. Cover the opening of the jar with a clean cotton cloth and hold it in place with a rubber band. Place your jar in a warm spot (72°F to 78°F) out of direct sunlight and leave your kombucha undisturbed to ferment for 7 days.

Taste your kombucha, using a straw. Does it taste too sweet? Let it go a few more days before tasting again. Is it sufficiently tart and you love it? Great! Time for the next step.

Carefully remove the SCOBY with rinsed hands and place it on a clean porcelain or glass plate or bowl bathed in kombucha. This will be your culture for the next batch. If you are immediately proceeding with another batch, reserve about 2 cups of the finished kombucha for the starter tea of your next brew. (Otherwise, to put your SCOBY to rest, see page 8.)

To flavor the kombucha, divide the ginger equally among the bottles (4 to 6 slices per 16-ounce bottle). Fill the bottles with the harvested kombucha using a spouted measuring cup (for an easy pour) and a plastic funnel, leaving about 1 inch of air space in the neck of the bottle. As you pour, you may want to use a fine-mesh strainer to filter out yeast strands. Cap tightly.

To begin the optional secondary fermentation, simply store the capped bottles in a warm dry place (72°F to 78°F is best) for 48 hours. Be aware that the sugars present will add fuel to the fermentation action in the bottle, which will increase the pressure inside the bottles. Chill one of the bottles for at least 6 hours. Crack it open and pour it into a glass. If it effervesces, you've done it! If you want more carbonation, let it go for a few more days and test again with another chilled bottle. When you're pleased with the carbonation, refrigerate all the bottles to end the fermentation. Strain when serving if desired.

VARIATION

Amp up this recipe by flavoring your water with fresh ginger. Thinly slice about 2 inches of peeled ginger. Boil the ginger slices in 2 cups of water for 10 minutes. Filter through a coffee filter to remove all ginger particles because they may interfere with the SCOBY. Substitute these 2 cups of ginger-flavored water for 2 cups of the water you'll be using to brew your tea. You can still add more ginger slices at the bottling stage.

POMEGRANATE KOMBUCHA

Pomegranates soared to popularity because of their high amount of antioxidants. The taste can range from sweet to sour depending on the variety of pomegranate and its ripeness, but as a general rule, if you like the taste of grenadine syrup, you probably like pomegranate. You can push this infusion to the sweeter side by adding more juice or make it more sour by using less.

MAKES 1 GALLON

14 cups purified water

16 to 20 tea bags or 8 tablespoons (35 grams) loose-leaf black tea

1 cup evaporated cane sugar

2 cups starter tea (see page 10)

1 SCOBY (see page 7)

4 cups pomegranate juice

Heat 6 cups of the water in a stainless steel saucepan to 212°F over medium heat. Remove from the heat, add the tea, stir well, and cover. Steep for 4 minutes, stirring once after 2 minutes. Remove the tea bags or pour the tea through a colander or fine-mesh strainer into a second pot. Compost the tea.

Add the sugar and stir until dissolved. Add the remaining 8 cups of water to cool the tea to about room temperature (72°F or cooler). Add 2 cups of the starter tea and stir. Pour into a 1-gallon jar.

With rinsed hands, carefully lay the SCOBY on the surface of the tea. Cover the opening of the jar with a clean cotton cloth and hold it in place with a rubber band. Place the jar in a warm spot (72°F to 78°F) out of direct sunlight and leave undisturbed to ferment for 7 days.

Taste your kombucha using a straw. Does it taste too sweet? Let it go a few more days before tasting again. Is it sufficiently tart, and you love it? Time for the next step.

Carefully remove the SCOBY with rinsed hands and place it on a clean porcelain or glass plate or bowl bathed in kombucha. This will be your culture for the next batch. If immediately proceeding with another batch, reserve about 2 cups of the finished kombucha for the starter tea of your next brew. (Otherwise, to put your SCOBY to rest, see page 8.)

continued

Pomegranate Kombucha, *continued*

Add the pomegranate juice to the fermented kombucha tea. Stir gently. Using a funnel and a spouted measuring cup (for easy pouring), fill your bottles with the flavored kombucha, leaving about 1 inch of air space in the neck of the bottle. As you pour, you may want to use a fine-mesh strainer to filter out yeast strands. Cap tightly. Your kombucha is ready to drink, but if you prefer a more carbonated beverage, proceed to the next step.

To begin the optional secondary fermentation process, simply store the capped bottles in a warm dry place (72°F to 78°F is best) for 48 hours. Be aware that the sugars present will add fuel to the fermentation action in the bottle, which will increase the pressure inside the bottles. After 48 hours, chill one of the bottles for at least 6 hours. Crack it open and pour it into a glass. If it effervesces, you've done it! If you want more carbonation, let it go for a few more days and test again with another chilled bottle. When you're pleased with the carbonation, refrigerate all the bottles to end the fermentation.

LAVENDER-GREEN TEA KOMBUCHA

Ahhh, the calming effect of lavender. The fragrance is known to relax and soothe the mind and the body. Meld with antioxidant-rich green tea, and you have a powerful formula designed to reduce stress and lift your spirits.

MAKES 1 GALLON

15 1/2 cups purified water

16 to 20 tea bags or 8 tablespoons (35 grams) loose-leaf black tea

1 cup evaporated cane sugar

2 cups starter tea (see page 10)

1 SCOBY (see page 7)

4 teaspoons chopped fresh lavender buds, or 2 teaspoons dried

Heat 6 cups of the water in a stainless steel saucepan over medium heat to 170°F, then remove from heat. Add the tea, stir well, and cover. Steep for 4 minutes, stirring once at 2 minutes. Remove the tea bags or pour tea through a colander or fine-mesh strainer into a second pot. Compost the tea.

Add the sugar and stir until dissolved. Then add 8 cups of water to cool the tea to about room temperature (72°F or cooler). Add the starter tea and stir. Pour into a 1-gallon jar.

With rinsed hands, carefully lay the SCOBY on the surface of the tea. Cover the opening of the jar with a clean cotton cloth and hold it in place with a rubber band. Place the jar in a warm spot (72°F to 78°F) out of direct sunlight and leave undisturbed to ferment for 7 days.

Taste the kombucha, using a straw. Does it taste too sweet? Let it go a few more days before tasting again. Is it sufficiently tart and you love it? Great! Time for the next step.

Carefully remove the SCOBY with rinsed hands and place on a clean porcelain or glass plate or bowl bathed in kombucha. This will be your culture for the next batch. If immediately proceeding with another batch, reserve about 2 cups of the finished kombucha for the starter tea of your next brew. (Otherwise, to put your SCOBY to rest, see page 8.)

continued

Lavender–Green Tea Kombucha, *continued*

To steep the lavender, put the buds in a suitable tea ball, cheesecloth, or loose-leaf tea brewing device. Bring the remaining $1^1/_2$ cups of water to a boil.

Use $^1/_2$ cup of the hot water to warm the container in which you'll steep the lavender. Pour it off.

Add the lavender to the container. Pour the hot water over, cover, and allow to steep for 5 minutes, but no longer than 5 minutes; lavender can go bitter. Remove the lavender and allow to cool to room temperature.

Using the funnel and spouted measuring cup (for easy pouring), divide the lavender infusion equally among the bottles (about 2 tablespoons per 16-ounce bottle). Fill the bottles with the green tea kombucha, leaving 1 inch of air space in the neck. As you pour, you may want to use a fine-mesh strainer to filter out yeast strands. Cap tightly.

To begin the optional secondary fermentation, simply store the capped bottles in a warm dry place (72°F to 78°F is best) for 48 hours. Be aware that the sugars present will add fuel to the fermentation action in the bottle, which will increase the pressure inside the bottles. After 48 hours, chill one of the bottles for at least 6 hours. Crack it open and pour into a glass. If it effervesces, you've done it! If you want more carbonation, let it go for a few more days and test another chilled bottle. When you're pleased with the carbonation, refrigerate all the bottles to end the fermentation.

GINGER RAIL KOMBUCHA

This infusion gives ginger ale a run for its money. Dry and crisp with a real ginger kick, it is followed by a mellow minty afterglow for a potent yet pleasant refreshment. MAKES 1 GALLON

14 cups purified water

16 to 20 tea bags or 8 tablespoons (35 grams) loose-leaf black tea

1 cup evaporated cane sugar

2 cups starter tea (see page 10)

1 SCOBY (see page 7)

1/2 cup dried ginger, sliced

6 tablespoons chopped fresh mint leaves

Heat 6 cups of the water in a stainless steel saucepan to 212°F over medium heat, then remove from the heat. Add the tea, stir well, and cover. Steep for 4 minutes, stirring once at 2 minutes. Remove the tea bags or pour the tea through a colander or fine-mesh strainer into a second pot. Compost the tea.

Add the sugar and stir until dissolved. Add the remaining 8 cups of water to cool the tea to about room temperature (72°F or cooler). Add the starter tea and stir. Pour into a 1-gallon jar.

With rinsed hands, carefully lay your SCOBY on the surface of the tea. Cover the opening of the jar with a clean cotton cloth and hold it in place with a rubber band. Place the jar in a warm spot (72°F to 78°F) out of direct sunlight and leave undisturbed to ferment for 7 days.

Taste your kombucha using a straw. Does it taste too sweet? Let it go a few more days before tasting again. Is it sufficiently tart and you love it? Great! Time for the next step.

Carefully remove the SCOBY with rinsed hands and place it on a clean porcelain or glass plate or bowl bathed in kombucha. This will be your culture for the next batch. If immediately proceeding with another batch, reserve about 2 cups of the finished kombucha for the starter for your next brew. (Otherwise, to put your SCOBY to rest, see page 8.)

continued

Ginger Rail Kombucha, *continued*

Divide the ginger and mint equally among the bottles. Fill with kombucha using a spouted measuring cup (for an easy pour) and a plastic funnel, leaving about 1 inch of air space in the neck of the bottle. As you pour, you may want use a fine-mesh strainer to filter out yeast strands. Cap tightly.

To begin the optional secondary fermentation, simply store the capped bottles in a warm dry place (72°F to 78°F is best) for 48 hours. Be aware that the sugars present will add fuel to the fermentation action in the bottle, which will increase the pressure inside the bottles. After 48 hours, chill one of the bottles for at least 6 hours. Crack it open and pour it into a glass. If it effervesces, you've done it! If you want more carbonation, let it go for a few more days and test again with another chilled bottle. When you're pleased with the carbonation, refrigerate all the bottles to end the fermentation. Strain when serving if desired.

MIX IT

Fill a collins glass with ice. Add 2 ounces (1/4 cup) Ginger Rail Kombucha and 2 ounces (1/4 cup) vodka or other clear, neutral alcohol. Add a splash of club soda, and a sprig of mint and a lime wedge for garnish. Stir and enjoy.

LAVENDER-LEMONADE KOMBUCHA

As delicious as it is healing, this infused kombucha combines the refreshing flavor of fresh lemon juice with the calming properties of lavender. The flavor is unique and beautiful—sweet with floral notes. MAKES 1 GALLON

14 cups purified water

8 to 10 tea bags or 4 tablespoons (18 grams) loose-leaf black tea

8 to 10 tea bags or 4 tablespoons (18 grams) loose-leaf green tea

1 cup evaporated cane sugar

2 cups starter tea (see page 10)

1 SCOBY (see page 7)

$1/2$ cup lemon juice (about 4 lemons)

12 teaspoons fresh or 4 teaspoons dried lavender blossoms

Heat 6 cups of the water in a stainless steel saucepan to 212°F over medium heat, then remove from the heat. Add the tea, stir well, and cover. Steep for 4 minutes, stirring once at 2 minutes. Remove the tea bags or pour the tea through a colander into a second pot. Compost the tea. Add the sugar and stir until dissolved. Add the remaining 8 cups of water to cool the tea to about room temperature (72°F or cooler). Add the starter tea and stir. Pour into a 1-gallon jar.

With rinsed hands, carefully lay your SCOBY on the surface of the tea. Cover the opening of the jar with a clean cotton cloth and hold it in place with a rubber band. Place the jar in a warm spot (72°F to 78°F) out of direct sunlight and leave undisturbed to ferment for 7 days.

Taste your kombucha using a straw. Too sweet? Let it go a few more days. Is it sufficiently tart and you love it? Great! Time for the next step. Remove the SCOBY with rinsed hands and place on a clean porcelain or glass plate bathed in kombucha. This will be your culture for the next batch. If immediately proceeding with another batch, reserve 2 cups of the finished kombucha for the starter tea for your next brew. (To put your SCOBY to rest, see page 8.)

For the secondary fermentation, divide the lemon juice and lavender blossoms equally among the bottles (about 1 table-spoon juice and 1½ teaspoons fresh lavender per 16-ounce bottle). Fill the bottles with the kombucha using a spouted measuring cup and a plastic funnel, leaving about 1 inch of air space in the neck of the bottle. As you pour, you may want use a fine-mesh strainer to filter out yeast strands. Cap tightly. Let the bottles ferment at room temperature (about 72°F) for 48 hours. Refrigerate and enjoy! Strain when serving if desired.

HOLIDAY SPICE KOMBUCHA

Leaves turning colors, pumpkins adorning doorsteps, pillowy white snow drifts, and the scent of cinnamon herald the holiday season. Here's a fun alternative to conventional spiced cider with the added benefit of being a health tonic for the entire family to enjoy. The blueberries give the kombucha a festive bluish-red tint, while the cinnamon and cardamom add a spicy note to dazzle your senses. MAKES 1 GALLON

14 cups purified water

8 to 10 tea bags or
4 tablespoons (18 grams)
loose-leaf black tea

8 to 10 tea bags or
4 tablespoons (18 grams)
loose-leaf green tea

1 cup evaporated
cane sugar

2 cups starter tea
(see page 10)

1 SCOBY (see page 7)

32 fresh or frozen
blueberries

4 cinnamon sticks

8 cardamom pods

Holiday Spice Kombucha,
glass and back bottle;
Lavender-Lemonade
Kombucha (page 35),
center bottle

Heat 6 cups of the water in a stainless steel saucepan to 212°F over medium heat, then remove from the heat. Add the tea, stir well, and cover. Steep for 4 minutes, stirring once at 2 minutes. Remove the tea bags or pour the tea through a colander or fine-mesh strainer into a second pot. Compost the tea.

Add the sugar and stir until dissolved. Add the remaining 8 cups of water to cool the tea to about room temperature (72°F or cooler). Add the starter tea and stir. Pour into a 1-gallon jar.

With rinsed hands, carefully lay your SCOBY on the surface of the tea. Cover the opening of the jar with a clean cotton cloth and hold it in place with a rubber band. Place the jar in a warm spot (72°F to 78°F) out of direct sunlight and leave undisturbed to ferment for 7 days.

Taste your kombucha using a straw. Does it taste too sweet? Let it go a few more days before tasting again. Is it sufficiently tart and you love it? Great! Time for the next step.

Carefully remove the SCOBY with rinsed hands and place on a clean porcelain or glass plate or bowl bathed in kombucha. This will be your culture for the next batch. If immediately proceeding with another batch, reserve about 2 cups of the finished kombucha for the starter tea of your next brew. (Otherwise, to put your SCOBY to rest, see page 8.)

continued

Holiday Spice Kombucha, *continued*

For the secondary fermentation, divide the blueberries, cinnamon sticks, and cardamom pods equally among the bottles (4 blueberries, ½ cinnamon stick, and 1 cardamom pod per 16-ounce bottle). Fill the bottles with the kombucha using a spouted measuring cup (for an easy pour) and a plastic funnel, leaving about 1 inch of air space in the neck of the bottle. As you pour, you may want use a fine-mesh strainer to filter out yeast strands. Cap tightly.

Let the bottles ferment at room temperature (about 72°F) for 48 hours. Refrigerate and enjoy! Strain when serving if desired.

BLACK JACK KOMBUCHA

Sweet notes of caramel, a hint of tropical fruit, and a smooth vanilla finish with just the right amount of dryness and effervescence is what's in store for your taste buds with this unique infusion. Using maple syrup instead of sugar will slightly darken the color of the kombucha and impart a subtle maple flavor. Don't settle for anything less than Madagascar vanilla beans, which boast a rich, dark, and creamy flavor, and sweet, buttery aromatic qualities. MAKES 1 GALLON

14 cups purified water

16 to 20 tea bags or
8 tablespoons (35 grams)
loose-leaf black tea

4 tablespoons finely
chopped dried pineapple

2 tablespoon finely ground
toasted dried coconut

2 Madagascar vanilla
beans, finely chopped

2 cups Grade B maple syrup

2 cups starter tea
(see page 10)

1 SCOBY (see page 7)

Heat 6 cups of the water in a stainless steel saucepan to 212°F over medium heat, then remove from the heat. Add the tea, stir well, and cover. Steep for 4 minutes, stirring once at 2 minutes. Remove the tea bags or pour the tea through a colander or fine-mesh strainer into a second pot. Compost the tea.

Add the dried pineapple, coconut, and vanilla bean. Add the maple syrup and stir until dissolved. Add the remaining 8 cups of water to cool the tea to about room temperature (72°F or cooler). Add the starter tea and stir. Pour into a 1-gallon jar.

With rinsed hands, carefully lay your SCOBY on the surface of the tea. Cover the opening of the jar with a clean cotton cloth and hold it in place with a rubber band. Place the jar in a warm spot (72°F to 78°F) out of direct sunlight and leave undisturbed to ferment for 7 days.

Taste your kombucha using a straw. Does it taste too sweet? Let it go a few more days before tasting again. Is it sufficiently tart and you love it? Great! Time for the next step.

continued

Carefully remove the SCOBY with rinsed hands and place it on a clean porcelain or glass plate or bowl bathed in kombucha. This will be your culture for the next batch. If you are immediately proceeding with another batch of the same flavored kombucha, reserve about 2 cups of that kombucha for the starter tea of your next brew. (If you are proceeding with brewing a different kombucha—flavored or not—this flavored batch should not be used. To put your SCOBY to rest, see page 8.)

Fill your bottles with the kombucha using a spouted measuring cup (for an easy pour) and a plastic funnel, leaving about 1 inch of air space in the neck of the bottle. As you pour, you may want use a fine-mesh strainer to filter out yeast strands and the pine-apple, coconut, and vanilla beans. Cap tightly.

To begin the optional secondary fermentation, simply store the capped bottles in a warm dry place (72°F to 78°F is best) for 48 hours. Be aware that the sugars present will add fuel to the fermentation action in the bottle, which will increase the pressure inside the bottles. After 48 hours, chill one of the bottles for at least 6 hours. Crack it open and pour it into a glass. If it effervesces, you've done it! If you want more carbon-ation, let it go for a few more days and test again with a chilled bottle. When you're pleased with the carbonation, refrigerate all the bottles to end the fermentation. Strain when serving if desired.

MIX IT

Pour 2 ounces ($^1/_4$ cup) Black Jack Kombucha in a tall glass and add 2 ounces ($^1/_4$ cup) bourbon, whiskey, or dark rum. Add a splash of club soda and a twist of orange to garnish. Stir and enjoy.

BAMBUCHA

I love bamboo. I grow it in my backyard, and I appreciate it as the most sustainable building material in the world. When I learned that a company in my hometown of Portland, Oregon, manufactures and sells handcrafted bamboo products like cutting boards and utensils—and brews their own kombucha—I just had to find out more about these folks. Their infusion BambuCha (a clever combination of their company name, Bambu, and "cha," which means tea in Chinese) has become a favorite of mine, with its berry-based sweetness and ginger-chile kick. If you like, add healthy chia seeds for a "bubble-tea" effect. MAKES 1 GALLON

14 cups purified water

10 to 12 tea bags or 5 tablespoons (20 grams) loose-leaf white tea

6 to 8 tea bags or 3 tablespoons (15 grams) loose-leaf black tea

1 cup evaporated cane sugar

2 cups starter tea (see page 10)

1 SCOBY (see page 7)

2 cups strawberries, sliced

2 cups goji berries

2 tablespoons peeled and grated fresh ginger

2 small chiles, seeded and diced

1/2 cup chia seeds, hydrated (optional; see page 42)

Heat 6 cups of the water in a stainless steel saucepan to 212°F over medium heat, then remove from the heat. Add the tea, stir well, and cover. Steep for 4 minutes, stirring once at 2 minutes. Remove the tea bags or pour the tea through a colander or fine-mesh strainer into a second pot. Compost the tea.

Add the sugar and stir until dissolved. Add the remaining 8 cups of water to cool the tea to about room temperature (72°F or cooler). Add the starter tea and stir. Pour into a 1-gallon jar.

With rinsed hands, carefully lay your SCOBY on the surface of the tea. Cover the opening of the jar with a clean cotton cloth and hold it in place with a rubber band. Place your jar in a warm spot (72°F to 78°F) out of direct sunlight and leave undisturbed to ferment for 7 days.

Taste your kombucha using a straw. Does it taste too sweet? Let it go a few more days before tasting again. Is it sufficiently tart and you love it? Great! Time for the next step.

continued

Bambucha, *continued*

Carefully remove the SCOBY with rinsed hands and place on a clean porcelain or glass plate or bowl bathed in kombucha. This will be your culture for the next batch. If immediately proceeding with another batch, reserve about 2 cups of the finished kombucha for the starter tea of your next brew. (Otherwise, to put your SCOBY to rest, see page 8.)

Divide the strawberries, goji berries, ginger, chiles, and chia equally among the bottles. Fill the bottles with the kombucha using a spouted measuring cup (for an easy pour) and a plastic funnel, leaving about 1 inch of air space in the neck of the bottle. As you pour, you may want use a fine-mesh strainer to filter out yeast strands. Cap tightly.

For the optional secondary fermentation, simply store the capped bottles in a warm dry place (72°F to 78°F is best) for 48 hours. Be aware that the sugars present will add fuel to the fermentation action in the bottle, which will increase the pressure inside the bottles. After 48 hours, chill one of the bottles for at least 6 hours. Crack it open and pour it into a glass. If it effervesces, you've done it! If you want more carbonation, let it go for a few more days and test again with another chilled bottle. When you're pleased with the carbonation, refrigerate all the bottles to end the fermentation. Strain when serving if desired.

CHIA SEEDS

Chia seeds are packed with omega-3s, antioxidants, fiber, and protein. To prepare, soak 1/2 cup in 1 cup water for about 20 minutes, stirring occasionally to keep the seeds from clumping. The result will be a chia gel that can be added to your kombucha during bottling (before the secondary fermentation). You can also add it to a kombucha cocktail, vinegar, or sauce right before enjoying.

KOMBUCHA ROOT BEER SASPARILLA

A legendary nonalcoholic drink ordered in saloons across the Old West, sasparilla (or sarsaparilla) has been called the granddaddy of all root beers, although the modern beverage flavor is closer to a mixture of sassafras and birch oil. Like kombucha, sasparilla has been heralded as a tonic for well-being. Call it what you want, but try this twist on an old favorite. Or as the cartoon character Yosemite Sam says, "Sasparilly, and make it snappy!" Ingredients such as sasparilla, burdock, and sassafras can be found in specialty markets or online shops like Frontier Co-op or even Amazon. You can substitute brown sugar for the sorghum and $^1/_2$ cinnamon stick for the cinnamon chips, if you prefer. MAKES 1 GALLON

14 cups purified water

12 tea bags or
6 tablespoons (28 grams)
loose-leaf black tea

$^1/_4$ cup dried sasparilla root

1 teaspoon cinnamon chips

4 teaspoons diced dried
burdock root

4 teaspoons diced dried
sassafras root bark

1 cup sorghum extract

$^1/_4$ cup evaporated cane
sugar

2 cups starter tea
(see page 10)

1 SCOBY (see page 7)

Combine the water, tea, sasparilla root, cinnamon chips, burdock, and sassafras in a stainless steel saucepan. Bring to a boil, let boil for 5 minutes, stirring occasionally, and turn off heat.

Mix in the sorghum and sugar and cool to about room temperature (72°F or cooler), about 2 hours.

Strain the liquid and discard the solids. Add the starter tea. Pour into a 1-gallon jar.

With rinsed hands, carefully lay your SCOBY on the surface of the tea. Cover the opening of the jar with a clean cotton cloth and hold it in place with a rubber band. Place in a warm spot (72°F to 78°F) out of direct sunlight and leave undisturbed to ferment for 7 days.

Taste your kombucha using a straw. Does it taste too sweet? Let it go a few more days before tasting again. Is it sufficiently tart and you love it? Great! Time for the next step.

Carefully remove the SCOBY with rinsed hands and place it on a clean porcelain or glass plate or bowl bathed in kombucha. This will be your culture for the next batch. If immediately proceeding with another batch of the same flavored kombucha, reserve about 2 cups of that kombucha for the starter tea of your next brew. (If you are proceeding with brewing a different kombucha—flavored or not—do not use this kombucha as the starter tea. To put your SCOBY to rest, see page 8.)

Fill the bottles with the harvested kombucha using a spouted measuring cup (for an easy pour) and a plastic funnel, leaving about 1 inch of air space in the neck of the bottle. As you pour, you may want to use a fine-mesh strainer to filter out yeast strands. Cap tightly.

To begin the optional secondary fermentation, simply store the capped bottles in a warm dry place (72°F to 78°F is best). Be aware that the sugars present will add fuel to the fermentation action in the bottle, which will increase the pressure inside the bottles. After 48 hours, chill one of the bottles for at least 6 hours. Crack it open and pour it into a glass. If it effervesces, you've done it! If you want more carbonation, let it go for a few more days and test again with another chilled bottle. When you're pleased with the carbonation, refrigerate all the bottles to end the fermentation process.

BLUE EYES

In all of my tea roving, I have yet to be bored by the seemingly infinite combinations of teas, flowers, and botanicals. What you may also discover is that it's even more fun to ferment them! This inventive infusion is one of my favorites. It's the brainchild of Rich Awn, who founded Mombucha in his Brooklyn apartment and delivers bottles by bicycle. One day, he discovered a fruity herbal blend called "Blue Eyes" at The Garden market just around the corner of his house, and was inspired to work it into a kombucha. The result is pleasantly sweet, fruity, and floral. You can find dried rose hips and dried hibiscus flowers at specialty spice stores or online at SavorySpiceShop.com or Kalustyans.com. MAKES 1 GALLON

14 cups purified water

16 to 20 tea bags or
8 tablespoons (35 grams)
loose-leaf black tea

2 cups pure grade B maple
syrup

2 cups starter tea
(see page 10)

1/2 cup fresh rhubarb, or
1/4 cup dried rhubarb

2 tablespoons dried
rose hips

2 tablespoons dried
hibiscus flower

1 SCOBY (see page 7)

Heat 6 cups of the water in a stainless steel saucepan to 212°F over medium heat, then remove from the heat. Add the tea, stir well, and cover. Steep for 4 minutes, stirring once after 2 minutes. Pour the tea through a colander or fine-mesh strainer into a second pot. Compost the tea.

Add the maple syrup and stir until dissolved. Then add the remaining 8 cups of water to cool the tea to about room temperature (72°F or cooler). Add 2 cups of the starter tea and stir. Pour into a 1-gallon jar. Add the rhubarb, rose hips, and hibiscus.

With rinsed hands, carefully lay your SCOBY on the surface of the tea. Cover the jar's opening with your clean cotton cloth holding it in place with a rubber band. Place your jar in a warm spot (72°F to 78°F) out of direct sunlight and leave your kombucha undisturbed to ferment for 7 days.

Taste your kombucha using a straw. Does it taste too sweet? Let it go a few more days before tasting again. Is it sufficiently tart and you love it? Great! Time for the next step.

Carefully remove the SCOBY with rinsed hands and place it on a clean porcelain or glass plate or bowl bathed in kombucha. This will be your culture for the next batch. If immediately proceeding with another batch of the same flavored kombucha, reserve about 2 cups of that kombucha for the starter tea of your next brew. (If you are proceeding with brewing a different kombucha—flavored or not—do not use this kombucha as the starter tea. To put your SCOBY to rest, see page 8.)

Fill your bottles with the flavored kombucha using a spouted measuring cup (for an easy pour) and a plastic funnel, leaving about 1 inch of air space in the neck of the bottle. Some prefer to filter at this step with a fine-mesh strainer to filter out yeast strands and the rhubarb, rose hips, and hibiscus. Cap tightly.

To begin the optional secondary fermentation, simply store the capped bottles in a warm dry place (72°F to 78°F is best). Be aware that the sugars present will add fuel to the fermentation action in the bottle, which will increase the pressure inside the bottles. After 48 hours, chill one of the bottles for at least 6 hours. Crack it open and pour it into a glass. If it effervesces, you've done it! If you want more carbonation, let it go for a few more days and test again with another chilled bottle. When you're pleased with the carbonation, refrigerate all the bottles to end the fermentation.

MIX IT

Fill a collins glass with ice. Add about 1 tablespoon of fresh blueberries so they disperse evenly among the ice cubes. Add 2 ounces (1/4 cup) Blue Eyes kombucha. Fill the remainder of the glass with club soda, stir, and garnish with a slice of star fruit for an impressive mocktail.

Chapter 2

JUICES AND SMOOTHIES

Tart, effervescent kombucha blends perfectly with fruit juice and fresh produce and turns ordinary drinks into beverages of distinction. Especially in spring and summer, I look forward to adding fresh berries and different kinds of fruits and vegetables. I prefer a more drinkable smoothie (not too thick), and kombucha helps thin blended drinks while still contributing to their flavor and health value. I also enjoy experimenting with the look and texture of my juice drinks. Kombucha can brighten up the dark leafy green of kale, complement the tangy red of cranberry, and provide a bright counterpoint to the earthiness of yellow turmeric. Blending kombucha with juices, fruits, vegetables, herbs, and spices makes me feel like I'm getting all my daily doses of the good stuff my body needs, while enjoying a rainbow of colors and flavors.

POMEGRANATE-CRANBERRY COMBO

Did you know pomegranate juice has more antioxidants ounce-for-ounce than green tea or red wine? Or that cranberry juice is considered a natural defense against heart disease? While I appreciate these good-for-me juices and do like to drink each one straight, sometimes the tartness can be over-powering. Try blending these two bright red juices with my Pomegranate Kombucha for a milder, more balanced drink. Although this recipe makes just enough for one, feel free to make more for when friends drop by—larger batches can be stored in the refrigerator, tightly capped, for up to a week.
SERVES 1

$^1/_2$ cup Pomegranate
Kombucha (page 29)

$^1/_4$ cup pomegranate juice

2 tablespoons frozen
cranberry juice concentrate

Splash of freshly squeezed
lime juice

Skewered fresh cranberries
(optional garnish)

Blend the kombucha, pomegranate juice, and cranberry juice concentrate together. Pour into a glass. Add splash of lime and garnish if desired.

SMOOTH RECOVERY

This concoction will help when you are feeling a little rough around the edges from the night before. Kick-start your morning with something cool, healthy, refreshing, and energizing. Flax seeds provide an omega-3 boost, while hemp seeds, which may be one of the healthiest foods in the world, add omega-6 fatty acids and are an excellent source of protein. The banana and strawberries provide the smooth texture for an easy-to-drink breakfast food.

SERVES 1

1 cup strawberries

1 banana

1 tablespoon ground flax

1 tablespoon raw hemp seeds

1 tablespoon raw wheat germ

1 cup Pomegranate Kombucha (page 29)

1/2 cup ice

In a blender or food processor, mix strawberries and banana together. Add the flax, hemp seeds, wheat germ, and kombucha. Blend on high until smooth and creamy, 30 to 60 seconds. Serve over ice and enjoy.

GINGER-PEACH BLACK TEA

Some people like ginger-infused tea. Others like their peach-flavored iced tea. This perfect combination of the two can be served either hot or cold, depending on the time of year and your mood. Using black tea kombucha (page 19) provides the boldness while the pressed raw ginger adds the zing. **SERVES 2**

2 cups plain black tea kombucha (page 19)

1 cup peach juice (or nectar)

4-inch knob of ginger, peeled

In a glass, mix kombucha and peach juice together. With a garlic press, squeeze the ginger to add just the juice into the mixture. Add more ginger if a stronger flavor is desired. Stir and serve.

SNAPPY APPLE

If you like drinks with a bit of heat, you're going to love this apple-jalapeño combo. The jalapeño pepper has been grown for centuries in Veracruz, Mexico. When shopping for this solid green pepper, make sure it is firm and smooth-skinned; avoid the ones that are soft, bruised, or have wrinkled skin. To dial down the amount of heat, remove the veins and seeds from the jalapeño before juicing. And, did you know the chipotle pepper, which is a staple of Tex-Mex cuisine, is just a ripe jalapeño that's been smoked? Try one in place of the jalapeño for a smoky flavor. SERVES 2

1 jalapeño

2 cups plain kombucha (page 19)

1 cup apple juice

1/2 teaspoon freshly squeezed lemon juice

2 tablespoons honey

To make the jalapeño juice, put a whole jalapeño in a juicer or blender and process. Remove and measure out 1/4 teaspoon of juice (discard the rest). Combine the jalapeño juice, kombucha, apple juice, lemon juice, and honey in a blender. Blend for 5 to 10 seconds until well mixed. Pour into a glass. Olé!

INSTANT PICK-ME-UP

You're at work, it is three o'clock in the afternoon, and you've hit the proverbial wall. Instead of loading up on coffee or an energy drink, consider a healthy cold beverage that will reinvigorate you naturally. The dash of cayenne pepper not only wakes up the senses, it also helps regulate blood flow to get your motor running again. The result is more physical energy and mental acuity. SERVES 1

2 cups plain kombucha (page 19)

¹/₄ teaspoon ground turmeric

¹/₄ teaspoon cayenne pepper

1 slice cucumber, to garnish

Ice (optional)

Mix together the kombucha, turmeric, and cayenne pepper. Stir. Garnish with a cucumber wheel to cool you off. Shoot it back or serve over ice and sip slowly for a gradual energy buzz.

SWEET BEET

Pull out your juicer to make this fresh combination, or simply buy the juices to make this sweet and tangy blend with a subtle ginger flavor. SERVES 2

1¹/₂-inch knob peeled
fresh ginger

1¹/₂ cups plain kombucha
(page 19)

¹/₂ cup freshly squeezed
orange juice

¹/₂ cup carrot juice

¹/₂ cup beet juice

2 teaspoons freshly
squeezed lemon juice

Combine the ginger, kombucha, orange juice, carrot juice, beet juice, and lemon juice in a blender and blend for about 15 seconds. Note: There will be small pieces of ginger. Strain through a fine-mesh strainer to remove the ginger pieces, if desired. Serve.

SUPREME GOODNESS KOMBUCHA DRINK

There's a lot of green goodness in this healthy juice drink. Feel free to experiment with this basic recipe by adding a little yogurt for a velvety texture or topping it off with crumbled nuts such as walnuts or pecans. SERVES 2

2 celery stalks

$^1/_2$ cucumber, peeled

$^1/_2$ cup apple juice (or about 2 apples, cored and peeled)

$^1/_2$ cup stemmed and chopped kale

$^1/_2$ cup chopped spinach

$^1/_3$ cup chopped cilantro leaves

1 cup plain kombucha (page 19)

1 teaspoon freshly squeezed lemon juice

Prepare the celery for juicing by cutting off both ends of the stalks and using just the middle part. Juice the celery and cucumber in a juicer. If you are using fresh apples, juice them as well. Combine the kale, spinach, cilantro, kombucha, and juices into a blender. Blend for about 15 seconds. Serve and enjoy!

BLOOD ORANGE ITALIAN SODA

It's amazing how fast the kombucha industry has been growing since I started Kombucha Wonder Drink in 2001. Part of the reason is thanks to educators and master brewers, such as Hannah Crum, the "Kombucha Mamma" and founder of KombuchaKamp.com, who are serving as teachers and resources to inspire home brewers. Here's Hannah's take on Blood Orange Italian Soda, which usually employs simple syrup. Her healthier twist harvests savory notes of basil and thyme to offset the gentle sweetness of fresh blood oranges, creating an infusion with delicious, bold flavor and often overflowing natural fizz. Slicing the herbs helps release the healthy volatile oils and anti-inflammatory flavonoids from the basil and thyme, which then are infused into the brew. SERVES 1

2 to 4 tablespoons freshly squeezed blood orange juice (from 1/2 to 1 blood orange)

3 to 4 fresh basil leaves, sliced, or 1/2 teaspoon dried basil

1 sprig fresh thyme, sliced, or 1/2 teaspoon dried thyme

2 cups plain kombucha (page 19)

Using a funnel, pour the blood orange juice into a 16-ounce bottle. Add the basil and thyme, then fill to the top with kombucha. Seal tightly, store at room temperature (about 72°F) for 2 to 3 days, and taste daily until it reaches the flavor you enjoy. You can strain out the brewing herbs before serving. To best maintain your customized flavor, store in the refrigerator.

MIX IT

For a creative twist, make a Blood Orange Kombucha Italian Cream Soda by adding 1 tablespoon of cream and a splash of soda water. Or try a Blood Orange Kombucharita by mixing 4 parts Blood Orange Kombucha Italian Soda with 1 part tequila. Garnish with a fresh leaf of thyme and of basil and a slice of orange.

VEGGIE DELIGHT

This savory tomato blend is complemented well by the sweet tartness of kombucha. Sprinkle a dash of hot sauce to give a bit of a spicy kick. SERVES 2

6 tomatoes, or 1¹/₂ cups tomato juice

¹/₂ green bell pepper

¹/₂ red bell pepper

4 celery stalks

¹/₂ cup chopped green onion, green parts only

¹/₂ cup chopped cilantro leaves

¹/₂ cup plain kombucha (page 19)

³/₄ teaspoon kosher salt

Hot sauce

Combine the tomatoes, green pepper, red pepper, celery, green onion, and cilantro in a juicer and juice. Mix the vegetable juice with the kombucha in a pitcher. Add the salt and hot sauce. Serve and enjoy!

MIX IT

Add a shot of vodka for an excellent Bloody Mary. Serve on the rocks and garnish with a celery stem.

MAPLE-ALMOND SMOOTHIE

This hearty smoothie is great for sustaining energy. It is perfect for breakfast or before exercising. In addition to its own health benefits, the kombucha provides a pleasant lightness to a nutrient-dense drink. SERVES 2

1 cup plain kombucha, plus more as needed (page 19)

1/2 cup almond butter

1 tablespoon Grade B maple syrup

1 banana

Combine all of the ingredients in a blender. Blend until smooth, about 10 seconds. Add more kombucha to taste, if desired. Serve and enjoy!

BLUEBERRY SMOOTHIE

I have pleasant memories of picking blueberries in the summer at my aunt's farm in Mulino, Oregon, when I was a kid. I would pick a couple of those ripe juicy berries, eat one; pick three, eat two; and so on until my hands and face were dyed blue, my pail was full to the brim, and I had blueberries coming out of my ears (at least that's what my aunt told me). Now I enjoy filling a martini glass with blueberries and enjoying them as a healthy dessert. Or I'll make this recipe as a meal when I want something light on a hot summer day.
SERVES 2

1 cup plain kombucha
(page 19)

1 cup blueberries

³/₄ cup Greek yogurt

2 tablespoons honey

Combine all of the ingredients in a blender. Blend until smooth, about 10 seconds. Serve and enjoy.

LEMONADE BERRY BLAST SMOOTHIE

Antioxidant-packed blueberries are the second-most consumed berry in America (after strawberries). They're also one of the few fruits native to North America, so enjoy this homegrown superfood in a tart and tangy smoothie featuring lemonade and kombucha. You'll be a hit at the family picnic or a hero at your backyard barbecue. A great refreshing drink ideal for warm weather. SERVES 2

1 cup plain kombucha
(page 19)

1 cup lemonade

1 cup frozen blueberries

1 banana

2 cups ice cubes

Fresh mint, to garnish

Combine the kombucha, lemonade, blueberries, banana, and ice in a blender and blend until smooth. Pour the thick cold smoothie into two tall glasses and serve each with a sprig of fresh mint. Keep refrigerated if you do not drink it all. It will be hard not to do so.

ABLE & BAKER'S BLASTOFF
FRUITION SMOOTHIE

Upon returning to Earth after surviving space travel, legend has it the pioneering primates Able and Baker communicated in sign language not that they were "happy to be back," but told their handlers, "If it was not for this morning's kombucha smoothie, we would not have lived." With vitamin D and bioflavonoids from the kale, antioxidants from the blueberries, polyphenols from the tea, vitamins C, B_1, B_2, B_6, B_{12}, a cargo of amino acids, terrific avocado fat, and lots of real fiber, the Able & Baker puts zero gravity in your morning pursuit. SERVES 2

1 cup raw kale, stemmed

1 orange, peeled

1 cup blueberries

1 ripe avocado

$1^1/_2$ to 2 cups plain kombucha (page 19)

Combine the kale, orange, blueberries, avocado, and $1^1/_2$ cups of the kombucha in blender. Mix until thoroughly combined. Add the reserved $1/_2$ cup kombucha as needed for desired consistency.

GREEN SMOOTHIE

Kale is king. This superstar leafy vegetable is everywhere—in salads, dried as chips, and, of course, blended in smoothies. Like its "K" cousin, kombucha, kale promotes regular digestion and helps balance the good bacteria in your gut. In addition to a panoply of healthy fruits, I like to add bee pollen to this smoothie, which is a natural remedy for seasonal allergies like hay fever. And, like kombucha, bee pollen is said to enhance energy. SERVES 2

1 cup plain kombucha
(page 19)

Juice from 1/2 lemon

3 bananas

1 apple, cored and peeled

1 pear, cored and peeled

2 cups stemmed and
chopped kale

1 teaspoon bee pollen
(optional)

Combine the kombucha and lemon juice in a blender. Add the bananas, apple, pear, kale, and bee pollen. Blend and serve.

BABY'S PAW

For centuries, explorers have set out to find the mythical Fountain of Youth. If that's you, Seeker, look no further. Through the magic of the universe's first age-reversing smoothie, cosmic forces have combined to create the Baby's Paw, a legendary wrinkle-reducing concoction made with the island gift of supple young coconut flesh and its precious white water. Add the eternal strawberry and your favorite age-old kombucha. For best results, drink daily. SERVES 1

Flesh of one young coconut

1/2 cup young coconut water

1 cup frozen strawberries, stemmed

1/2 cup plain oolong kombucha (page 19)

2 teaspoons honey or Grade B maple syrup (optional)

Remove the top of a young coconut. Carefully reserve the coconut juice. With a spoon, scrape out the interior of the coconut, removing as much flesh as possible. Combine the coconut flesh, coconut water, strawberries, kombucha, and honey in a blender. Pulse until well mixed. Pour into a glass and enjoy.

KOMBUCHA OVER THE RAINBOW

Somewhere a leprechaun sits on a pot of gold sipping a smoothie as nutrient-dense and mouth-wowing as this colorful morning glory. Because this is a smoothie packed with so much goodness, don't be surprised if your outer aura emanates red, green, and blue from drinking one on a cloudy day. Note: If using yellow kiwis, you can leave the skin on. It's edible and good for you.

SERVES 2

1 golden beet, with greens

1 green apple

$^1/_2$ cup fresh cilantro leaves

Juice of 1 lime

$1^1/_2$ cups plain kombucha (page 19)

2 kiwis

$^1/_2$ teaspoon chopped fresh peeled ginger

1 cup frozen raspberries

$^1/_2$ cup Greek yogurt (optional)

In a juicer, juice the beet, apple, and cilantro. Combine with the lime juice and kombucha. Gently stir and set aside. In a blender, blend the kiwis, ginger, raspberries, and yogurt. Pour in the kombucha mixture and blend until thoroughly combined, about 30 seconds. Serve.

Chapter 3

SPIRITED COCKTAILS

Kombucha is a great mixer, particularly for cocktails. I enjoy kombucha with a simple splash of bitters and vodka, but the world of kombucha cocktails certainly doesn't stop there. Kombucha is on the move from tea and coffee shops to restaurants and bars, as patrons eschew sugary syrups and bartenders experiment with artisanal ingredients. But your desire for a healthier lifestyle—while still enjoying a delicious cocktail now and then—can also be accomplished at home. By substituting kombucha as a mixer in many alcoholic beverages, some might say you're able to detox while you drink. Enjoy experimenting with these cocktails—and sharing them with your friends.

SIMPLE SYRUP

Simple syrup is an essential item to stock in any bar where sweetened cocktails are made. As the name implies, it is very easy to make. Simple syrup is typically used in place of raw sugar, and allows flexibility depending on how sweet you like your drink. You can make a "rich" simple syrup by doubling the amount of sugar, or you can make what is commonly know as "bar" simple syrup, which is the recipe here.

Water

Evaporated cane sugar

Bring 1 part water to a boil and add 1 part sugar, stirring constantly. When the sugar is completely dissolved, remove the pot from the heat. Allow the mixture to cool and thicken. Bottle and store in the refrigerator. If well sealed, simple syrup can last for several months.

GOMME (GUM) SYRUP

The main difference between simple syrup and gomme syrup is gomme syrup uses an emulsifier to add a silky texture to many classic cocktails. You can buy gomme syrup in the specialty drink section of natural foods stores, or you can order it online. You can also make your own; you just have to find gum arabic, which is also available at natural foods stores or online. The reason some bartenders use gomme syrup is that it can soften the flavor of alcohol-heavy cocktail classics like an old-fashioned.

Water

Gum arabic

Evaporated cane sugar

Combine 1 part water and 1 part gum arabic and bring to a boil, stirring constantly until the gum arabic is completely dissolved. Allow the mixture to cool. Make a "rich" simple syrup by combining 2 parts water and 4 parts sugar and bring to a boil, stirring constantly until the sugar is completely dissolved. Add the gum arabic mixture and bring to a boil. Stir the boiling mixture continually for about 2 minutes. Bottle after cooling. Store in refrigerator. If well sealed, gomme syrup can last for several months.

IMPOSSIBLE DREAM

It may be impossible to dream of a sweeter, more sublime fruit cocktail than this silky smooth spin on a classic cocktail. You could get lost in the pool of its subtle orange hues, especially if you toast the occasion with the setting sun as your backdrop. The bite of the lime juice is offset by the creaminess of the apricot liqueur; and the tanginess of the kombucha marries well with the juniper overtones of the gin. Instead of using simple syrup, try gomme (or gum) syrup to soften the alcohol flavor. But watch out, this clever cocktail could just as well have been called the "Impossible to Stop." SERVES 1

3¹/₂ tablespoons
(1³/₄ ounces) gin

¹/₄ cup (2 ounces) plain
kombucha (page 19)

1 tablespoon (¹/₂ ounce)
freshly squeezed lime juice
(about ¹/₂ of a lime)

1 tablespoon (¹/₂ ounce)
apricot liqueur

Dash gomme syrup
(page 73)

Crushed ice

Lime slice, to garnish

Combine the gin, kombucha, lime juice, apricot liqueur, and gomme syrup in a collins glass. Fill with crushed ice and mix. Serve garnished with a lime wheel.

YERBA BUENA

This "good herb" cocktail comes from Edgar Tamayo and Jonathan Ojinaga of Azúcar Lounge in San Francisco, which is well known for its Latin-inspired cocktails. With curative kombucha plus lavender and gin, you'll be feeling *muy bueno.* SERVES 1

2 to 3 fresh herb sprigs (rosemary, oregano, and sage or other herbs of your choice)

3 tablespoons (1½ ounces) gin

2 tablespoons (1 ounce) freshly squeezed lime juice (about 1 lime)

2 tablespoons (1 ounce) simple syrup (page 73)

Ice

3 tablespoons (1½ ounces) Lavender–Green Tea Kombucha (page 31)

Muddle 1 to 2 sprigs of a fresh herb in a mixing glass. Add the gin, lime juice, and simple syrup. Fill the glass with ice. Shake for approximately 15 seconds. Strain into a collins glass filled with ice. Float the Lavender–Green Tea Kombucha on top. Garnish with the remaining sprig of fresh herb.

OLD WEST

Who can forget cowboy Alan Ladd sidling up to the bar in an old Western saloon with his six-shooter . . . and ordering a sasparilla in the movie *Shane*? (Though one would have to be of a certain age like this author to have actually seen the movie when it came out in 1953.) It is my favorite movie, and this could be my favorite drink. I love how the ginger, kombucha, and root beer flavors meld with the bourbon. An ideal cocktail for watching a great Western. SERVES 1

2-inch knob peeled fresh ginger

4 mint leaves

3 tablespoons (1¹/₂ ounces) plain kombucha (page 19)

3 tablespoons (1¹/₂ ounces) sasparilla

2 tablespoons (1 ounce) bourbon

Crushed ice

2 tablespoons (1 ounce) club soda

Place the ginger and 2 of the mint leaves in the bottom of a cocktail shaker and press with a muddler or blunt kitchen instrument. Add the kombucha, sasparilla, and bourbon. Shake. Strain the contents into a collins glass filled with crushed ice. Top with club soda. Give the cocktail a light stir and garnish with the remaining mint leaves.

THE PETTICOAT

This drink may be feminine in nature with its dressing of St. Germain elderflower liqueur, but this take on the well-known gin and tonic can pack a punch when you least expect it. Pump up the fizz in your kombucha for this one. She's sweet, but strong! SERVES 1

Ice

¹/₄ cup (2 ounces) gin

3 tablespoons (1¹/₂ ounces) St. Germain elderflower liqueur

¹/₂ to 1 cup plain kombucha (page 19)

1 teaspoon simple syrup (page 73)

Fill a collins glass with ice. Add the gin, St. Germain, kombucha, and simple syrup. Stir and enjoy.

HEALTHY MULE

Ginger: spicy, pungent, aromatic, and good for the gut. Does it get any better? Perhaps—if it is slyly mixed with fizzy kombucha and ice-cold vodka. The Moscow Mule is typically a ginger beer, vodka, and lime cocktail, served in a copper mug. Go kombucha-style with a ginger brew and lemon to create a tart "healthy mule" that pulls its weight on a warm summer night. SERVES 1

Ice

¹/₂ cup (4 ounces) Ginger Kombucha (page 26)

3 tablespoons (1¹/₂ ounces) vodka

Squeeze of lemon juice

Cucumber slice, to garnish

Sprig of fresh basil

Drop 3 large ice cubes into a collins glass or copper mug. Add the kombucha and vodka. Add the lemon juice and garnish with a cucumber wheel and fresh basil. Serve with a stirring rod.

MOONSHINE COCKTAIL

Jovial King of Urban Moonshine is an expert when it comes to pairing food and drink with bitters, which are made of a variety of herbs, fruits, spices, and roots distilled in a base liquor. She inspired me to add cherry bitters to my Traditional Kombucha Wonder Drink—and what a wonderfully refreshing flavor combination! Try this re-creation of a classic cocktail and enjoy the digestive benefits of both kombucha and bitters. The dashes of bitters lend an aromatic, well-balanced flavor to the fresh citrus, resulting in a crisp cocktail. I recommend using Urban Moonshine's Citrus Bitters. SERVES 1

2-inch peeled fresh ginger, chopped

Ice

1 tablespoon ($1/2$ ounce) freshly squeezed lime juice (about $1/2$ of a lime)

1 tablespoon ($1/2$ ounce) freshly squeezed lemon juice (about $1/4$ of a lemon)

6 tablespoons (3 ounces) plain kombucha (page 19)

6 tablespoons (3 ounces) vodka

5 dashes bitters

Twist of lemon peel, to garnish

Place the ginger in the bottom of a cocktail shaker and press with a muddler or blunt kitchen utensil. Half fill the shaker with ice. Add the lime juice, lemon juice, kombucha, vodka, and bitters. Shake well. Pour the strained liquor into a chilled martini glass and garnish with a twisted peel of lemon.

SEANZ KAFKA

The Czech Republic may be famous for its beer, but the country also produces some interesting and unique alcoholic beverages. They make a bitter herb liqueur called Becherovka, which is widely available in America. If you want, you can experiment with making your own version by adding bitters and other natural herbs to a base liqueur. This intense cocktail is inspired by Czech author Franz Kafka's brooding darkness, but it comes from somewhere close to home—Portland's very own Valentine's. SERVES 1

Ice

¹/₄ cup (2 ounces) bourbon

¹/₄ cup (2 ounces) Becherovka (or bitter herb liqueur)

Dash of freshly squeezed lemon juice

Ginger Kombucha (page 26)

Fill a collins glass with ice. Add the bourbon, Becherovka, and lemon juice and stir. Finish with a float of the ginger kombucha. Enjoy!

INTERNATIONAL ELDER

Legend has it Saint Germain had the power of longevity. A lot of people feel that way about kombucha as well, so double the goodness by combining these two elixirs into one potent drink. The St. Germain elderflower liqueur pairs well with most distilled spirits and is a perfect complement to champagne or white wine. SERVES 1

Ice

3 tablespoons (1½ ounces) champagne or sparkling white wine

3 tablespoons (1½ ounces) St. Germain elderflower liqueur

3 tablespoons (1½ ounces) club soda

6 tablespoons (3 ounces) plain kombucha (page 19)

Twist of lemon peel, to garnish

Fill a collins glass with ice. In this order, add the sparkling wine, St. Germain, club soda, then kombucha. Stir. Add a twist of lemon and serve.

SWEET ITALIAN

Heavily influenced by two Italian distilled spirits, this gin cocktail has sweet undertones, yet offers a boozy, burly depth that complements kombucha's vinegary bite. *Amaro* means "bitter" in Italian and is packed with herbs and spices. Aperol has a sweeter flavor, with hints of mandarin orange. The two liqueurs combine for a bittersweet flavor that is unique and complex. And to prove kombucha isn't always austere, top this vibrant orange cocktail with a cherry. SERVES 1

¹/₄ cup (2 ounces) plain kombucha (page 19)

3 tablespoons (1¹/₂ ounces) gin

1 tablespoon (¹/₂ ounce) Amaro liqueur

1¹/₂ teaspoons (¹/₄ ounce) Aperol

Ice

1 Amarena cherry

In a mixing glass, combine the kombucha, gin, Amaro, and Aperol. Add ice and stir gently with a bar spoon. Fill a collins glass with ice, and top with an Amarena cherry. Strain ingredients from mixing glass over Amarena cherry into the glass.

CITRUS SUNSHINE MARTINI

Did you know that a tangerine is a mandarin orange, but not all mandarin oranges are tangerines? Okay, now that's cleared up. Mandarin oranges are sweeter than their other citrus cousins, have a bright orange skin that is easy to peel, and inner segments that are easily separated. Splash in some kombucha, mango puree, triple sec—and *voilà*—a bright, naturally sweet, and delicious cocktail the color of sunshine. For an extra mandarin burst, try mandarin-infused vodka. SERVES 1

Ice

1/4 cup (2 ounces) vodka

1 tablespoon (1/2 ounce) Triple Sec

1 1/2 teaspoons (1/4 ounce) plain kombucha (page 19)

1 1/2 teaspoons (1/4 ounce) fresh mango puree

Juice of 1 mandarin orange or a juicy navel orange

Twist of orange peel, to garnish

Chill a martini glass with ice cubes and set aside until the drink is prepared. Half fill a martini shaker with ice. Add the vodka, Triple Sec, kombucha, mango puree, and orange juice. Stir or lightly shake the mixture. Remove the ice from the martini glass, then pour the mixture through a strainer into the chilled martini glass. Add twist of orange peel to garnish.

CRANBERRY BITTERS COCKTAIL

Many people associate cranberries with autumn—it's what we serve at Thanksgiving. Well, here's a cranberry-flavored drink that celebrates my native Oregon coast's big, colorful cranberries year-round, especially on a hot summer night. It sets up well with the tartness of cranberry liqueur and kombucha, and then finds balance with the citrus and bitters. The St. Germain serves to smooth out the drink, but only after some vigorous shaking. No stirring here. SERVES 1

3 dashes Peychaud's Bitters

¹/₄ cup (2 ounces) plain kombucha (page 19)

2 tablespoons (1 ounce) St. Germain elderflower liqueur

1 tablespoon (¹/₂ ounce) cranberry liqueur

Ice

Twist of lemon peel, to garnish

In a mixing glass, combine 3 long dashes of bitters (more than 3 if the dashes are short), kombucha, St. Germain, and cranberry liqueur. Fill the glass with ice, top with a shaking tin and shake vigorously, I mean vigorously. Strain into an iced collins glass and garnish with a lemon twist, first squeezing the twist, and circling the rim with it for oil.

LONG KOMBUCHA ICED TEA

There has been some debate about the origin of the name of the Long Island Iced Tea, but pretty much everybody knows there's no iced tea in most variations of the famous cocktail. So, we lay claim to a more accurate title, which indeed features tea—specifically, citrus-infused kombucha. This drink goes down smoothly, especially on an outdoor patio on a hot afternoon, but be aware—it still packs a punch. SERVES 1

1 tablespoon
(1/2 ounce) Triple Sec

1 tablespoon
(1/2 ounce) light rum

1 tablespoon
(1/2 ounce) gin

1 tablespoon
(1/2 ounce) vodka

1 tablespoon (1/2 ounce)
tequila

2 tablespoons (1 ounce)
freshly squeezed lemon
juice

1 teaspoon evaporated
cane sugar

1/2 cup (4 ounces) Citrus
Kombucha (page 24)

Ice

Lemon wedge, to garnish

Mix together the Triple Sec, rum, gin, vodka, tequila, lemon juice, sugar, and kombucha. Serve in a collins glass with ice. Garnish with a lemon wedge on the edge of the glass. Enjoy!

GINGERED PEARBUCHA

The next generation of culinary professionals are doing really inventive things with kombucha, and due to my love of all things ginger, I just had to share this creation from Geoff Millner at our local Oregon Culinary Institute. It combines the spiciness of ginger with the succulence of a ripe pear. You can cut the natural sweetness the pear adds to the brandy by adjusting the amount of lemon juice you add. Ratchet up the impact by sourcing a pear-in-the-bottle from Oregon's Clear Creek Distillery, which they make with the traditional Alsace technique of growing a pear inside a bottle right in the orchard. SERVES 1

¼ cup (2 ounces) pear brandy

½ cup (4 ounces) Ginger Kombucha (page 26)

1½ tablespoons (¾ ounce) simple syrup (page 73)

1 tablespoon (½ ounce) freshly squeezed lemon juice

Ice

Lemon slice, to garnish

Mix the brandy, kombucha, simple syrup, and lemon juice in a cocktail shaker with ice. Strain into a highball glass filled with ice. Garnish with a lemon slice.

KOMBUCHA PEACH DAIQUIRI

Here's an umbrella-worthy cocktail for lounging in a hammock on a sandy beach (or in your own backyard). Think slushy peachy sweetness with a bit of tartness from the orange juice. The kombucha adds the tang, rounding out this delicious daiquiri. And if you want a refreshing mocktail for all ages, simply forgo the vodka and rum. SERVES 4

6 medium fresh peaches, skinned and pitted (or 20 ounces canned peaches, sliced)

4 tablespoons evaporated cane sugar

2 tablespoons frozen orange juice concentrate

$^1/_2$ cup (4 ounces) vodka

$^1/_2$ cup (4 ounces) dark rum

1 cup (8 ounces) plain kombucha (page 19)

2 cups ice

Add the peaches, sugar, orange juice concentrate, vodka, rum, and kombucha to a blender. Blend until well mixed, about 5 seconds. Add additional alcohol and sugar to taste, if desired. Add ice and blend until smooth. Divide into 4 glasses and serve.

BLUEBERRY MOJITO MOCKTAIL

This refreshing blueberry mojito is packed with antioxidants, which makes it perfect for combating all that sun exposure from those long summer afternoons on the patio. Its probiotic properties also make it a major mood booster—no alcohol needed here! SERVES 1

1 cup blueberries

2 tablespoons (1 ounce) freshly squeezed lemon juice (about 1/2 lemon)

1/4 cup mint leaves

1 tablespoon (1/2 ounce) Grade B maple syrup

1/2 cup ice

1/2 cup (4 ounces) water

1/3 cup (2²/3 ounces) plain kombucha (page 19)

In a blender, mix together blueberries, lemon, mint, maple syrup, ice and water. Blend until it forms a slushy consistency. Pour into a tall glass and stir in kombucha.

SEASONAL SANGRIA

Sangria, which has its roots in Spain, is popular because it's easy to make and is noted for its "anything goes" ingredients. Try this seasonal approach by adding plums or peaches in the spring and summer, or add grapes or apples in the fall and winter. Whatever the season or the reason, kombucha provides the "bubbly" to this fruit-based sangria. SERVES 4

22 ounces (2³/₄ cups) dry red wine

1 tablespoon evaporated cane sugar

1 orange, sliced

1 lemon, sliced

1 large stone fruit (plum, peach, apricot, and so on), pitted and cut into chunks

Juice of 1 orange

Juice of 1 lemon

³/₄ cup (6 ounces) club soda

2 cups (16 ounces) plain kombucha (page 19)

Ice

Combine the wine, sugar, orange, lemon, stone fruit, orange juice, and lemon juice in a serving pitcher and stir. Let sit refrigerated overnight. When it's time to serve, add the club soda and kombucha. Ladle into cups with ice.

Chapter 4

DRESSINGS AND DUNKS

For thousands of years, people have been using kombucha as a staple in their home for all kinds of uses. In my travels, I've heard lots of stories about the healing properties of kombucha, particularly relating to gut health, and especially when consumed on a regular basis. People tell me they feel better, have more energy, don't get sick as often, and on and on. I believe it's the "good bacteria" that aid digestion. I want to find more ways to incorporate kombucha in my daily diet because I have a sense of well-being when I regularly consume it. While I usually drink 8 ounces of Kombucha Wonder Drink in the morning and again in the afternoon, I've been inspired by many creative foodies—especially in the Pacific Northwest brewing and culinary world where I live—who are finding innovative ways to include kombucha in salad dressings, sauces, dips, marinades, and spreads. Here are some of my favorites.

KOMBUCHA MUSTARD

Here's another recipe for your well-fermented kombucha. And you can customize this one to fit your family's taste by adding any type and amount of spices, herbs, and sweeteners. Mustard is one of the most popular and widely used condiments in the world, but some like it hot, others sweet, yellow, brown, with seeds, and so on. By using different amounts of kombucha, you can make your mustard as thin or thick as you want.

If well fermented, more kombucha can be added to give the mustard more tang. To make it sweeter mustard, try adding anise or cinnamon and a bit of honey; to make it hotter, try ginger, cloves, horseradish, or black pepper.

MAKES ABOUT 2 CUPS

$^1/_2$ cup whole mustard seeds

Pinch of coarse ground sea salt (optional)

1 cup Kombucha Vinegar (page 96)

Herbs, spices, honey, prepared horseradish

Fill a glass jar (pint canning jars work well) or ceramic crock about half full with the mustard seeds. Add the salt. Add as much of the kombucha vinegar as needed to cover the seeds by about $^1/_2$ inch. Cover the container loosely with a lid, towel, or paper coffee filter. Store in a cool, dry place. Check the mustard seeds periodically and add more kombucha as necessary to keep the seeds covered and moist. As the seeds absorb the kombucha, they will swell, and it is important to keep them sufficiently moist. After a week or two, the seeds will be soft and will pop when you bite them. At this point, the seeds are ready for the blending stage but can continue to sit and ferment for up to a month if desired, provided they are kept moist.

Once the seeds are sufficiently soft, use a food processor or blender to blend the mixture to the desired consistency. Add herbs and spices to the mustard-kombucha mixture. Taste and adjust the seasoning. The mustard can be stored for 2 to 4 weeks in the refrigerator.

KOMBUCHA VINEGAR

If your unfinished home-brewed kombucha slips away from you and is well on its way to becoming vinegar, don't throw it out. Why not just let it become vinegar? Because kombucha is such a robust, aggressive culture and antioxidant, it can transition rather quickly to vinegar if the fermentation process is not stopped at the right time. So, don't fight it. There are lots of recipes in which you can use your own homemade vinegar in place of other cooking vinegars. Since the SCOBY from your batch of vinegar could imbue a harsh taste in any subsequent batch of kombucha, I recommend either discarding it or designating it as a "vinegar SCOBY" if you want to keep brewing vinegar. MAKES 1 SCANT GALLON

14 cups purified water

16 to 20 tea bags; or 8 tablespoons (35 grams) loose-leaf black tea or green tea, 6 tablespoons (35 grams) balled oolong tea, or 10 tablespoons (35 grams) loose open-leaf oolong tea

1 cup evaporated cane sugar

2 cups starter tea (see page 10)

1 SCOBY (see page 7)

Heat 6 cups of the water in a stainless steel saucepan to 212°F, then remove from the heat. Add the tea, stir well, and cover. Steep for 4 minutes, stirring once at 2 minutes. Remove the tea bags or pour the tea through a colander or fine-mesh strainer into a second pot. Compost the tea. Add the sugar and stir until dissolved. Then add the remaining 8 cups of water to cool the tea to about room temperature (72°F or cooler). Add the starter tea and stir. Pour into a 1-gallon jar. With rinsed hands, carefully lay your SCOBY on the surface of the tea. Cover the opening of the jar with a clean cotton cloth and hold it in place with a rubber band.

Place your jar in a warm spot (72°F to 78°F) out of direct sunlight and leave your kombucha undisturbed to ferment. A kombucha's vinegary nature is subject to taste. If you allow the fermentation to continue for 18 to 21 days (tasting it along the way with a straw), you should expect to make a basic vinegar. Age it for more than 3 to 5 weeks, and you will have a uniquely flavored product comparable to store-bought vinegar.

When the kombucha vinegar suits your taste, remove the SCOBY. Pour the liquid into a bottle and store in the refrigerator to cease the fermentation process.

KOMBUCHA DIPPING SAUCE

You can buy a good teriyaki dipping sauce at your local market, or you can try making it at home—with as much sweetness or heat as your taste buds desire. Use this sauce for dipping barbecued chicken, drizzling over salmon, drenching a lobster roll, pouring over steamed meat dumplings—or even dunking your hamburger and fries. MAKES ABOUT $3/4$ CUP

2 tablespoons teriyaki sauce

$1/2$ teaspoon minced fresh peeled ginger

$1/2$ teaspoon honey

$1^1/2$ teaspoons chili garlic sauce

$1/2$ cup Ginger Kombucha (page 26)

$1/4$ teaspoon sesame oil

Combine the teriyaki sauce, ginger, honey, chili garlic sauce, kombucha, and sesame oil. Stir until well blended. Store in the refrigerator for up to 2 weeks.

KOMBUCHA MIGNONETTE

My favorite place in Portland to get fresh oysters drizzled with their classic accompaniment, mignonette, is Park Kitchen, headed by chef-owner Scott Dolich. Traditionally, mignonette is made with champagne, white wine vinegar, black pepper, and diced shallots, but he suggested this variation, which substitutes kombucha for the champagne, and a tiny bit of cider vinegar for the white wine vinegar for a nice reddish hue. This piquant sauce provides a lovely balance to briny, somewhat creamy oysters. Why not try a dozen!

MAKES ABOUT $1/2$ CUP

$1/4$ cup plain kombucha (page 19)

2 tablespoons cider vinegar

2 tablespoons finely minced shallots

Freshly ground black pepper

Coarse ground sea salt

Combine the kombucha, vinegar, and shallots. Add a grind of black pepper and salt to taste.

KOMBUCHA VINAIGRETTE

Three parts oil to one part vinegar. Remember that and you're on your way to becoming a master vinaigrette maker. Oh, and don't forget that oil and vinegar will separate, so make sure you shake or stir your kombucha vinaigrette before serving. Once again, you'll want to use your well-fermented kombucha batch for this easy recipe. And feel free to enhance your vinaigrette with ingredients such as minced onion, garlic, herbs, salt, pepper, lemon, or honey for a dash of sweetness. MAKES 1 CUP

1/4 cup Kombucha Vinegar (page 96)

3/4 cup extra-virgin olive oil

1 teaspoon ground mustard seeds

Coarse ground sea salt

Freshly ground black pepper

Combine the kombucha vinegar with the olive oil, mustard, salt, and pepper to taste. Whisk together until combined. Pour over a salad or refrigerate in a sealed container for up to 1 week.

Kombucha Vinaigrette, bottom left; Mangobucha Tropical Dressing (page 102), top; Citrus Dressing (page 103), bottom right

MANGOBUCHA TROPICAL DRESSING

This easy-to-prepare tropical salad dressing sings with the rich flavor of the Ataulfo variety of mango, often called the champagne mango. This deep yellow oblong fruit, smaller in size than the more common reddish Tommy Atkins variety, is high in vitamin C and fiber. With its buttery flesh, it blends well with the garlic, ginger, oil, and citric juices. When you add your home-brewed green tea kombucha, the result is a gorgeous mango color (see photo, page 100) with a tropical fragrance and flavor ideal for all kinds of salads. My favorite combination for this dressing is with chopped kale, multicolored bell pepper slivers, avocado, sprouted sunflower seeds, and cooked lentils. If you don't have lemon-infused olive oil and don't want to infuse your own, you can substitute regular olive oil (or coconut oil) plus $^1/_2$ teaspoon finely grated lemon zest. MAKES 2 CUPS

3 cloves garlic

2-inch knob peeled fresh ginger

$^1/_2$ teaspoon coarse ground sea salt

$^1/_4$ teaspoon grains of paradise, ground (optional)

$^1/_2$ cup diced mango (champagne or Ataulfo variety preferred)

$^1/_2$ cup plain green tea kombucha (page 19)

$^1/_4$ cup freshly squeezed lime juice

$^1/_4$ cup freshly squeezed orange juice

2 tablespoons lemon-infused olive oil

In a food processor or blender, combine the garlic, ginger, salt, and grains of paradise and process until smooth, about 10 seconds. Add the mango and pulse until well mixed, about 10 seconds. Add the kombucha, lime juice, orange juice, and olive oil, and process until emulsified, about 1 minute. Chill and store in a sealed container in the refrigerator for up to 1 week

CITRUS DRESSING

Looking for the perfect dressing to brighten up your basic bowl of greens? This lovely and low-fat probiotic salad dressing has become a staple at my house. With a shelf life of up to 2 weeks, it may even get you to eat more salads. Feel free to add chopped fresh basil or your favorite seasonal herb to your new signature salad dressing. Make sure to use a blood orange if you want the vivid hue shown in the photo on page 100. MAKES 1 CUP

Juice from 1 large blood orange or juicy navel orange (about $^1/_2$ cup)

$^1/_2$ cup plain kombucha (page 19)

$^1/_4$ cup white balsamic vinegar

$^1/_4$ cup extra-virgin olive oil

$^1/_2$ teaspoon coarse ground sea salt

1 large clove garlic, minced

In a bowl, lightly whisk the orange juice, kombucha, balsamic vinegar, oil, salt, and garlic. Pour the salad dressing mixture into a cruet or mason jar with a secure lid. Keep refrigerated until you're ready to use it.

KOMBUCHA FIVE SPICE SYRUP

One might not think to serve Chinese five spice powder on ice cream, but once you prepare this kombucha syrup made by reducing kombucha, sugar, and the popular spice, you'll be looking for even more cold treats to pour it on. It's surprisingly thick, sweet, and spicy. Chinese five spice powder is commonly made from a combination of ground fennel seeds, Szechuan pepper, cloves, star anise, and cinnamon. It is often used in stir-fries and to add a complex sweetness to chicken, pork, duck, and vegetables dishes. In this case, save it for dessert. You won't be disappointed! MAKES 1/2 CUP

1³/₄ cups plain kombucha (page 19)

1/4 cup evaporated cane sugar

1/4 teaspoon Chinese five spice powder (recipe follows or use store-bought)

CHINESE FIVE SPICE POWDER

1 teaspoon ground cinnamon

1 whole star anise

16 whole cloves

1 teaspoon fennel seeds

1 teaspoon Szechuan peppercorns

Pour the kombucha into a small saucepan and simmer over medium heat until it is reduced by half, 15 to 20 minutes. Add the sugar and stir occasionally so sugar dissolves but doesn't burn. Simmer until reduced to 1/2 cup total volume, about 10 minutes. Add the spice and cook for 5 minutes. Strain through two layers of cheesecloth. Serve either warm or cool. If there is any left over, store covered in the refrigerator for up to 2 weeks.

To make the Chinese Five Spice Powder, toast the spices in a sauté pan over medium heat until fragrant, 4 to 7 minutes. Then grind them with a mortar and pestle (or in a coffee grinder used for spices) to make about 2 tablespoons of powder. Store extra in an air-tight container.

MIX IT

Use Kombucha Five Spice Syrup as a simple syrup in cocktails. Shake with whiskey, soda water, and a squeeze of lemon.

KOMBUCHA GINGER MARINADE

Kombucha marinade does wonders with chicken. It will help prevent the meat from drying out and also add extra flavor to the more delicate pieces—just make sure to separate the pieces to allow the maximum amount of marinade to reach as much of the meat as possible. Skinless, boneless chicken breasts can be marinated for as briefly as 30 minutes, while a whole chicken needs 6 to 8 hours. This recipe makes enough for either a split whole chicken or about 2 pounds of boneless chicken breasts or thighs. Place salt- and pepper-rubbed chicken in a shallow dish and cover with marinade; within 2 hours the chicken will be moist, flavorful, and ready to be grilled. MAKES ABOUT 2 CUPS

1 yellow onion, quartered

4-inch knob fresh peeled ginger, sliced

10 cloves garlic, peeled and separated

$1/4$ cup Vietnamese or Thai fish sauce

1 cup plain kombucha (page 19)

1 bunch cilantro

$1/4$ cup canola oil

Coarse ground sea salt

Freshly ground black pepper

In food processor, combine the onion, ginger, garlic, fish sauce, kombucha, cilantro, and canola oil. Blend until smooth. Add salt and pepper to taste. Can be stored in the refrigerator in an air-tight container for up to 1 week.

EDAMAME KOMBUCHA SPREAD

Mary Admasian at Aqua Vitea Kombucha, a Vermont-based kombucha micro-brewer, gave me this recipe for an edamame-based take on hummus, which has since found its way onto every type of edible snack in my house, including bread, pita chips, endive spears, celery stalks, and crackers. Sure, edamame is just a fancy name for boiled soybeans, but they sure do taste good, and this all-star legume is a great source of fiber, protein, vitamins, and minerals. If you like, you can substitute fresh basil for the cilantro. MAKES 2 CUPS

10 to 12 ounces frozen (shelled) edamame beans

1 cup plain kombucha, plus more as needed (page 19)

Juice of 1 lime

3 tablespoons extra-virgin olive oil

1 cup fresh cilantro leaves, chopped, plus more to garnish

2 cloves garlic, minced

1/2 teaspoon ground cumin

Sea salt, coarsely ground

Cook the edamame in a saucepan of boiling salted water until the beans are tender, 3 to 5 minutes. Drain and rinse in cold water until beans are cool.

In a food processor, combine the edamame, kombucha, lime juice, oil, cilantro, garlic, cumin, and salt to taste. Blend until smooth. Note: if mixture is too thick add a little more kombucha or water until you have a preferred consistency.

Transfer the dip to a bowl. Garnish the dip with a few sprigs of cilantro. Chill in the refrigerator for 1 to 2 hours. Serve cold.

VEGAN KOMBUCHA CHÈVRE SPREAD

People on a raw, vegan diet will naturally appreciate kombucha because it is a raw food that contains living enzymes. These enzymes, which are destroyed when food is heated over 116°F, assist in the digestion and absorption of food. This cashew and kombucha-based take on chèvre cheese pairs beautifully with fresh pears, figs, walnuts, and artisanal honey. Note that you'll need to soak the cashews ahead of time. SERVES 8

2 cups raw cashews

$^1/_2$ cup plain kombucha (page 19)

$^1/_4$ cup virgin coconut oil

1 tablespoon white miso paste

2 tablespoons debittered brewer's yeast flakes

1 teaspoon coarse ground sea salt (pink Himalayan salt suggested)

Fresh and/or dried herbs or flavorings, such as lavender, mint, lemon zest, thyme, or crushed peppercorns, for coating (optional)

Soak the cashews in water for at least 4 hours, then drain.

In a blender, combine the cashews, kombucha, oil, miso, yeast, and salt and process until smooth. Transfer the mixture to a clean airtight container. Allow the mixture to rest at room temperature for 24 hours. This will encourage the development of organic cultures, which gives the mixture its chèvre-like essence. Should you prefer a firmer "cheese," refrigerate for 2 to 4 hours before serving.

To make an herb-encrusted bûche de chèvre, begin by placing the "chèvre" on a piece of parchment and fold the parchment over itself. Now use the paper to pull the chèvre toward you to form a cylinder. Then oll the cylinder in the herb mix. Whether you prefer to leave the bûche de chèvre whole or slice it, refrigerate again briefly to allow it to set.

Chapter 5

KOMBUCHA AT THE TABLE

My wife and I like to entertain guests at our Oregon beach house, and one of my favorite weekend activities is to prepare a special dish for dinner—one that incorporates kombucha. Whether an appetizer, salad, side dish, or main course, I have fun starting with kombucha and seeing where I end up. Based on the positive receptions we've gotten, I would say more and more people are receptive to the unique flavor kombucha adds at the dinner table. I have purposely (and sometimes by mistake) let my kombucha rest too long, and it has crossed over to vinegar. This "well-fermented" kombucha, as I like to call it, actually works very well in many dishes that call for apple cider, vinegar, or pickling juice, and you can find instructions for how to make it on page 96. Simply bottle it in a fancy glass container with a spout and keep it in the kitchen. Add some high-quality extra-virgin olive oil and spices and pour liberally to experiment with the flavor on different fruits, greens, vegetables, and meats.

KOMBUCHA TROPICAL FRUIT SALAD

Everybody seems to be talking about coconut water. And why not? It's one of the most healthful drinks around. Many would say kombucha ranks right up there with coconut water as a beverage that promotes overall well-being. Use both in this tropical concoction brilliant with the bright green of the kiwi, orange of the mango, and the bold yellow of the papaya. Not to be confused with coconut milk, coconut water is tapped from young, green coconuts. The clear liquid from the fruit's center has a sweet, nutty taste. Substitute boxed coconut water if young, green coconuts are not available. SERVES 6

1/4 cup plain kombucha (page 19)

1/4 cup evaporated cane sugar

1/4 cup coconut water from a young, green coconut, strained

1 mango, peeled, seeded, and diced in large pieces

1 papaya, peeled, seeded, and diced

1 banana, peeled and diced

2 kiwis, peeled and diced

1 whole coconut, peeled and chopped

Combine the kombucha with the sugar and coconut water and set aside. In a bowl, mix together the mango, papaya, banana, kiwis, and coconut. Gently toss together until fruit is uniformly distributed. Add the kombucha–coconut water mixture to the fruit and toss together. Serve. Store any leftovers in a sealed container in the refrigerator for up to 2 days.

KOMBUCHA MUSHROOMS

Mushrooms and kombucha share a long history of being consumed for their health-promoting properties, especially in Asia where they both have been used medicinally for thousands of years. Kombucha also shares a special kinship with the much-loved fungus in that for eons kombucha was referred to as "mushroom tea." Well, kombucha is definitely not a mushroom, but the pale-looking "mother culture" used in the brewing process does bear a certain resemblance to the crown of a large mushroom. Bring these two old friends together and enjoy as a healthy snack or in a salad or wrap. Note that the mushrooms will need to marinate overnight. SERVES 6

5 ounces fresh whole shiitake mushrooms

1 tablespoon chili garlic paste

1 teaspoon minced fresh peeled ginger

1/4 cup soy sauce

1 cup plain kombucha (page 19)

1/2 teaspoon sesame oil

Combine the mushrooms, chili garlic paste, ginger, soy sauce, kombucha, and sesame oil in a resealable, refrigerator-safe container and let set overnight in the refrigerator before serving.

WILTED SPINACH WITH BACON-KOMBUCHA DRESSING

The heated bacon dressing wilts the spinach leaves and gives this salad a wonderfully delicate flavor. Spring is a fantastic time to make this salad. If you're thinking about a nice wine to accompany this dish, consider a rich chardonnay. SERVES 6

10 ounces fresh spinach, chopped

$^1/_4$ cup minced red onion

6 radishes, thinly sliced

2 to 4 slices thick-cut bacon

1 tablespoon evaporated cane sugar

3 tablespoons Kombucha Vinegar (page 96)

1 tablespoon water

$^1/_2$ teaspoon coarse ground sea salt

$^1/_8$ teaspoon freshly ground black pepper

2 hard-cooked eggs: 1 chopped, 1 sliced

Put the spinach in a large bowl. Add the onion and radishes.

Heat a skillet over medium-high heat. Add the bacon. When bacon slices start to curl, flip. Fry the bacon until crisp, 4 to 6 minutes. Transfer the bacon to a paper towel to drain. Set aside.

In the skillet, combine $1^1/_2$ to 2 tablespoons rendered bacon fat drippings with the sugar, vinegar, water, salt, and pepper. Heat until just boiling. Toss the chopped egg with the greens. Pour the hot dressing over greens mixture. Toss again lightly. Top with sliced egg and crumbled bacon and serve.

COMFORTING COLLARD GREENS IN KOMBUCHA

Collards are a substantial cruciferous green that provide a good amount of fiber. Adding kombucha to this classic Southern dish helps break down the greens and make the nutrients more bioavailable. And don't forget the corn bread to dip into your pot after preparation of this comfort food. Just don't overcook them because like other cruciferous vegetables they will emit an unpleasant sulfur smell if cooked too long. SERVES 4

1 pound collard greens

6 strips thick-cut bacon

1 yellow onion, chopped

2 to 3 cloves garlic, minced

1 tablespoon honey

$^1/_2$ teaspoon coarsely ground sea salt

$^1/_2$ teaspoon freshly ground black pepper

$^1/_4$ cup plain kombucha, plus more as needed (page 19)

1 cup vegetable broth (or water)

Remove the stems from the greens and discard. Slice the leaves into 3-inch strips. Set aside. Slice the bacon into small pieces.

Heat a large skillet over medium heat. Add the bacon and cook, stirring occasionally, until the edges are slightly browned, 2 to 4 minutes. Add the onion and cook until pieces become translucent and start to brown, 3 to 5 minutes. Add the garlic, honey, salt, and pepper and cook for about 1 minute. Add the kombucha, bring to a simmer, and cook until the liquid is reduced by half, about 3 minutes, stirring occasionally to keep bits from sticking to the pan.

Add the collards and broth to the pan and return to a simmer. Decrease the heat to medium-low and cook the collards until they are tender and have lost their brightness, about 20 minutes, stirring occasionally. Season to taste with more kombucha. Serve with the juices from the pan.

PASTA SALAD WITH KOMBUCHA HERB DRESSING

Karma Kombucha founder Susan Fink started out brewing in her kitchen, surrounded by SCOBYs and giant 30-gallon batches, so it's no wonder she found a way to work kombucha into a kitchen staple like pasta. This colorful take on pasta salad combines the zest of citrus and the kick of three fresh herbs: parsley, basil, and oregano. I like to make this for potlucks where I can talk up my secret ingredient: kombucha! SERVES 6

1 cup plain kombucha
(page 19)

Juice and zest of 1 orange
(about $1/4$ cup)

Juice and zest of 1 lemon
(about $1/3$ cup)

1 cup fresh parsley leaves

1 cup fresh basil leaves

1 tablespoon fresh
oregano leaves

$1/2$ cup extra-virgin olive oil

$1/2$ teaspoon coarsely
ground sea salt

$1/4$ teaspoon freshly
ground black pepper

1 pound penne pasta

$1/2$ cup shredded carrots

1 cucumber, peeled,
seeded, and diced

$1/2$ red or orange bell
pepper, diced

3 celery stalks, diced

Prepare the dressing by combining the kombucha, orange and lemon juices and zest, parsley, basil, and oregano in a blender or food processor and blending until pureed. While blending, slowly drizzle in the olive oil. Add salt and pepper.

Boil the pasta in plenty of salted water until al dente. Drain, then cool to room temperature.

In a large bowl, combine the pasta, carrots, cucumber, bell pepper, celery, and dressing. Toss and serve immediately or chill for a few hours before serving.

GREEN PAPAYA SALAD

The two papayas commonly grown are red and yellow in color, but pick either early, and it's called a green papaya. The unripe green fruit isn't sweet; it is actually kind of sour, which works well with the tanginess of kombucha in this ultimately savory dish. Combine with tastes common to Thai cuisine—fish sauce, hot chiles, salt, sugar, and sour lime—and you have a bowlful of complex flavors sure to please as a precursor to dinner or as an entrée that can stand alone. If available, you can substitute fresh Thai chiles for the chili paste. SERVES 4 TO 6

$^1/_2$ cup plain kombucha (page 19)

$^1/_2$ cup freshly squeezed lime juice

2 tablespoons Thai or Vietnamese fish sauce

1 tablespoon sambal olec chili paste

2 tablespoons lightly packed brown sugar

3 cloves garlic, thinly sliced

1 large green papaya, peeled and shredded or finely julienned

2 cups grape tomatoes, halved

1 bunch cilantro, coarsely chopped

$^1/_2$ cup macadamia nuts, chopped and toasted

Combine the kombucha, lime juice, fish sauce, sambal olec, brown sugar, and garlic in a bowl and mix. Add the papaya, tomatoes, cilantro, and macadamia nuts and toss until well mixed.

KOMBUCHA SUNOMONO

Oregon is home to many family farms, and one of my favorites is Kookoolan Farms operated by Chrissie and Koorosh Zaerpoor. It's where I learned about *sunomono,* a Japanese term for a variety of vinegared dishes, such as Japanese cucumber salad. Their version combines the tanginess of well-fermented kombucha and the sweetness of the soy and sugar into a very refreshing dish. Traditionally, these fresh pickles are made with rice wine vinegar, but kombucha vinegar has a depth of flavor that can't be matched by anything else, and the mirin adds a hint of sweetness. To dress up the dish and turn it into a more substantial meal, double the dressing and, after marinating the cucumbers for an hour, add $1/2$ cup of cooked, diced crab or shrimp and $1/4$ cup fresh chopped cilantro leaves and stir well. Serve over cold soba noodles, buckwheat noodles, or rice. SERVES 6

$1/2$ pound cucumber (about 1 large cucumber)

1 teaspoon coarse ground sea salt

2 tablespoons Kombucha Vinegar (page 96)

1 tablespoon evaporated cane sugar

1 teaspoon soy sauce or tamari

1 teaspoon toasted sesame oil

1 tablespoon mirin or sherry (optional)

Peel the cucumbers or not as you prefer; I use a carrot peeler to alternately remove the peel and leave the peel in place, resulting in a "striped" appearance. Slice the cucumber very thinly. Sprinkle the cucumber slices with salt, spread them out on paper towels, and leave for about 5 minutes. Squeeze out excess moisture by laying another paper towel on top of the slices and pressing with your open hands.

While the cucumbers are draining on the paper towels, combine the vinegar, sugar, soy sauce, sesame oil, and mirin in a bowl and mix well with a whisk. Add the cucumber and stir gently. Place the bowl in the refrigerator and refrigerate for at least 1 hour, and no more than 4 hours. To serve, place about 10 slices each on small individual dishes as a light appetizer or side dish.

KOMBUCHA TEA-BRINED EGGS

You can buy tea-brined eggs in pretty much every convenience store in Taiwan, but if a trip halfway around the world isn't on your agenda, try making this snack at home. By lightly cracking the shells before marinating, the result is a unique marbled pattern on the egg itself. The flavor is unique, too. While these are traditionally made with tea, using kombucha in the marinade adds a slightly sweet tang. Try adding brined eggs to soup (see Kombucha Ramen Noodles, page 124) or on a salad. MAKES 6 EGGS

6 eggs

2-inch knob fresh ginger

1 cup soy sauce

2 cups plain black tea kombucha (page 19)

$^1/_2$ stick cinnamon

2 star anise

1 teaspoon coarsely ground salt

5 cloves garlic, peeled and sliced

Cover the eggs with cold water in a saucepan. Bring to a boil. Remove from the heat, cover, and let sit for 10 minutes.

Meanwhile, char the ginger. Hold the knob with tongs directly over an open flame or place directly on a medium-hot electric burner. Slowly turn the ginger until the edges are slightly blackened and the ginger is fragrant, 3 to 4 minutes. Remove and discard the blackened peel and set aside.

Remove the eggs from the hot water and cool in a cold-water bath. Crack the eggs shells but do not remove from the egg.

Combine the soy sauce, kombucha, cinnamon stick, star anise, salt, garlic, and ginger in a small saucepan and bring to a boil. Put the cracked eggs in a bowl and pour the kombucha mixture over them. Marinate for 36 hours in the refrigerator, then remove the shell to reveal a dye pattern from the marinade. Serve sliced or eat whole.

HARVEST BREAKFAST BREAD WITH KOMBUCHA SOURDOUGH STARTER

When people ask me what kombucha is, I often respond by asking them if they're familiar with how sourdough bread is made. If they are, I usually don't have to provide much detail about the starter culture and the fermentation process—because both foods are produced in similar fashion and share a somewhat sour taste profile. Now you can experience both fermented products in one bread-making adventure. In this recipe, you'll be using the yeast that collects at the bottom of your jar plus the yeast strands you got by straining your kombucha when you bottled it—the yeast is what is left in the strainer. Typically, you should get enough yeast for this recipe from brewing one batch of kombucha, maybe two at the most. Note that you'll need to prepare your starter culture at least 24 hours ahead of time. MAKES 1 LOAF

4^1/$_2$ cups all-purpose flour, plus more if needed

1^1/$_2$ cups kombucha yeast threads

^{1}/$_2$ cup water, plus more if needed

^{1}/$_2$ cup plain kombucha, plus more if needed (page 19)

1 tablespoon coarsely ground sea salt

To make the sourdough starter, combine 1^1/$_2$ cups of the flour and all the kombucha yeast in a large bowl. Mix until combined (it will be lumpy). Note its size. Cover with a clean cotton cloth and let sit at room temperature (about 72°F) for 24 hours. Once bubbles have formed and it has doubled in size, you're ready to make the bread. If bubbles haven't formed and it hasn't doubled in size after 24 hours, mix in ^{1}/$_2$ cup flour and ^{1}/$_2$ cup kombucha mixed with 2 tablespoons of water. Let it sit for another 6 to 12 hours and check again. You may need to "feed it" one more time before it is ready.

When you're ready to make your dough, combine the full ball of starter you just made (about 3 cups) with the salt and ^{1}/$_2$ cup water. Mix until you no longer see the salt.

Slowly add the remaining 3 cups of flour bit by bit, using your hands. If the dough doesn't seem easy to work with, add $1/2$ cup more water. Knead the bread for 15 minutes on a lightly floured surface. Form into whatever shape loaf you prefer. Cut slits into the top. Place dough in an oiled pan or baking sheet.

Cover with a cloth and let rise for 6 to 12 hours, until doubled in size.

Preheat the oven to 350°F.

Bake for 1 hour. The crust will be golden in color and have a hollow sound when you tap on it. Cool in the pan for at least 5 minutes, then turn out onto a rack to continue cooling before slicing. Enjoy your homemade delicious kombucha sourdough bread all week.

KOMBUCHA LIME CEVICHE

Popular at tapas restaurants, ceviche can easily be made at home, too. Serve this kombucha version in fancy martini glasses garnished with slices of lime—perfect for a hot summer dinner gathering. You can select one kind of fish or use a variety, such as scallops, shrimp, halibut, flounder, or swordfish. While the lime juice "cooks" the fish—partially or completely, depending on how long it is marinated—make sure the seafood is very fresh because the citric acid does not kill bacteria and parasites as well as heat does. Note that the ceviche will need to marinate for several hours. SERVES 4

1 pound bay scallops (or another fish of your choice)

1 cup plain kombucha, plus more as needed (page 19)

Juice of 2 limes, plus more as needed

$^1/_2$ teaspoon coarsely ground sea salt

2 ripe tomatoes, diced

3 green onions, green and white parts, minced

2 stalks celery, diced

$^1/_2$ red bell pepper, minced

$^1/_2$ cup chopped fresh parsley

1 clove garlic, minced

2 tablespoons extra-virgin olive oil

2 tablespoons chopped fresh cilantro

Freshly ground black pepper or a dash of hot sauce

Rinse the scallops in cool water and place them in a medium bowl. Pour the kombucha and lime juice over the scallops. Add salt. The scallops should be completely immersed. Stir the mixture together gently. Chill the scallops for several hours until the scallops are opaque. (It is important that you cannot see through the scallops. This is how you know they are naturally cooked.) Remove half of the ceviche liquid from the bowl and discard. Keep the remaining liquid and add the tomatoes, green onions, celery, red pepper, parsley, garlic, olive oil, cilantro, and black pepper. Stir together. You may add more lime or kombucha to the final mixture if desired. Serve.

KOMBUCHA RAMEN NOODLES

Only an executive chef at one of the Pacific Northwest's best restaurants would think to combine kombucha with ramen noodles and elevate it with fresh ginger, garlic, mushrooms, and brussels sprouts. When Wildwood's Dustin Clark shared this recipe with me, I knew I'd have to pass it on . . . and blow away my old instant ramen noodle–loving college roommates. SERVES 6

KOMBUCHA BROTH

3-inch knob of ginger

1 onion

4-inch square kombu

6 cloves garlic

3 bay leaves

1 cup dried shiitake mushrooms caps

8 cups plain kombucha (page 19)

8 cups chicken stock

1/4 cup white miso

Dash of soy sauce

Char the ginger by holding the knob with tongs directly over an open flame or placing directly on a medium-hot electric burner. Slowly turn the ginger until the edges are slightly blackened and the ginger is fragrant, 3 to 4 minutes. Char the onion in the same way. Remove and discard the blackened peels and set aside.

To make the broth, combine the ginger, onion, kombu, garlic, bay leaves, mushrooms, kombucha, and chicken stock in a 6-quart stockpot. Bring to a boil, cover, and simmer for 45 minutes. Strain and reserve the shiitakes. Once cool enough to handle, slice the shiitakes into thin strips. Season the broth with the miso and soy sauce to taste.

To prepare the noodles, add noodles to a pot and add enough water to cover the noodles. Bring water to a boil and cook the noodles 4 to 7 minutes, until noodles are al dente. Drain and rinse. Combine with the stock.

To prepare the brussels sprouts, heat the olive oil in a skillet over medium heat. When the oil is hot, add the brussels sprouts. Sauté without stirring until golden brown, about 5 minutes. Stir them and let them cook until the other side is brown, another 3 to 5 minutes.

36 ounces dried ramen noodles, store bought or homemade

1 tablespoon extra-virgin olive oil

3 cups brussels sprouts, quartered

6 strips bacon

1 1/2 cups sliced green onions, green parts only

6 Kombucha Tea-Brined Eggs, peeled and sliced (page 119)

6 nori sheets, cut into 2-inch slices

To prepare the bacon, heat a skillet over medium-high heat. Add the bacon. When bacon slices start to curl, flip. Fry until crisp, 4 to 6 minutes. Transfer the bacon to a paper towel to drain. When cool, crumble or chop, then set aside.

To serve, divide the warm broth and ramen noodles among six bowls. Top each with 1/4 cup green onions, 1/2 cup brussels sprouts, 1 egg, bacon crumbles, and nori slices.

KOMBUCHA COLESLAW

There are many styles of coleslaw. There's a creamy version with buttermilk and mayonnaise; there's a red slaw that uses ketchup and vinegar; there's the original Dutch-style "koolsla," which loosely translates to cabbage salad; and (starting now) there's this kombucha-style slaw with toasted sesame seeds, tamari, and ginger root. However you make it, it's one of America's favorite salads, especially when served beside fried chicken at a Fourth of July picnic. This particular version is also perfect in the fish tacos on page 127. SERVES 6

$1/4$ cup plain kombucha (page 19)

$11/2$ teaspoons honey

1 teaspoon sesame oil

5 tablespoons canola oil

1 teaspoon tamari

1 tablespoon freshly squeezed lemon juice

1 tablespoon freshly grated peeled ginger

6 cups broccoli slaw mix (freshly grated broccoli stems, cabbage, and carrots)

1 cup chopped green onions, green parts only

Coarsely ground sea salt

Freshly ground black pepper

3 tablespoons sesame seeds

Make the dressing by combining the kombucha, honey, sesame oil, 3 tablespoons of the canola oil, tamari, lemon juice, and grated ginger.

In a separate bowl, mix together the slaw mix and green onions. Pour the dressing over the slaw mix and add salt and pepper to taste.

In a small saucepan or skillet, heat the remaining 2 tablespoons of canola oil over medium heat. Add the sesame seeds and toast for 2 to 5 minutes until they darken and become fragrant. Shake the pan occasionally to make sure the seeds don't stick to the pan. Watch them closely because they can burn quickly. Add to the salad. Mix and serve.

KOMBUCHA-BATTERED ALASKAN-COD FISH TACOS

You want to beer batter your fish for fish tacos, but open the refrigerator door, and alas, no beer. But because you have that bottle of kombucha next to the milk, you're in luck. Kombucha will work even better for this recipe because you can use it as an ingredient for the fish and the slaw. I like to use cod in my fish tacos, but any firm white fish (like halibut) will work. The kombucha slaw should provide a goodly amount of tanginess, but no reason not to add your favorite hot sauce. SERVES 6 TO 8

KOMBUCHA BATTER

1 cup all-purpose flour

1 teaspoon coarsely ground salt

$1/2$ teaspoon freshly ground black pepper

$1/2$ teaspoon baking powder

$1/4$ teaspoon cayenne

1 cup plain (page 19) or Citrus Kombucha (page 24)

1 teaspoon ground ginger

1 pound Alaskan cod

10 (6-inch) corn or flour tortillas

Canola oil, for frying

1 avocado, thinly sliced

4 cups Kombucha Coleslaw (page 126)

Cilantro leaves, removed from stems

Lemon wedges, to serve

Hot sauce, to serve (optional)

To prepare the batter, mix together the flour, salt, pepper, baking powder, and cayenne. Add the kombucha and ginger. Stir until ingredients are just mixed.

Pat the fish dry to remove excess moisture. Remove the skin and bones from the fish. Slice the fish into 2-inch pieces. Place the fish in the batter, coat well, and let stand for 15 minutes.

Preheat the oven to 170°F. Warm the tortillas for about 10 minutes.

Heat the oil in a deep fryer to 375°F. If you are pan frying, heat about 1 inch of canola oil in a large pan to 375°F. Place a few pieces of fish in the hot oil and fry until golden brown on one side, then flip to cook the other side, 2 to 4 minutes per side. Cook the fish in batches to maintain the oil temperature. Place fish on a drying rack to cool. Pat down with paper towels to remove excess oil.

Place two pieces of cod in the center of each tortilla. Lay some of the sliced avocado next to the fish. Add $1/4$ to $1/2$ cup of slaw on top. Sprinkle with a bit of cilantro. Squeeze a bit of lemon juice on top to enhance the flavor. To make a spicier version, add a bit of hot sauce. Serve and enjoy!

Chapter 6

SWEETS
AND ICES

I'll admit it . . . I have a sweet tooth. I love a bowl of ice cream or sorbet after dinner. It's a guilty pleasure made more palatable when I know one of the ingredients—kombucha—is good for me. Kombucha's consistency lends itself well to cool and frozen treats, and I've found it's one of the best ways to introduce kombucha to youngsters. They may not be ready for the unique tartness of some commercial kombucha beverages, but you might be surprised to discover how much children (and the young at heart) will enjoy the subtle and sweet undertones that flavor gelatin, sorbet, ice cream, floats, and snow cones.

KOMBUCHA JELL-O

No matter how old you are, making and eating Jell-O is downright fun. This recipe gives the neon Jell-O from our childhood a natural makeover by replacing the artificial colors and flavors with kombucha, which adds a wonderful, light tartness to your homemade gelatin. Play around using different flavors of kombucha or better yet, use your own concoctions! (See chapter 1 for my favorite infusion recipes to try.) Any mold will do; find a funny-shaped store-bought one or use a container you find around the house. Agar-agar can be used as a vegan substitute for gelatin (see below). SERVES 2 TO 4

1 cup cold water

1 (1-tablespoon) packet plain gelatin

¼ cup evaporated cane sugar

1 cup cold plain kombucha (page 19)

Put ¼ cup of the cold water in a small dish. Sprinkle the gelatin over the cold water to activate. Bring the remaining ¾ cup water to a boil in a small saucepan and take off the burner. Add the gelatin mixture and sugar to the hot water and stir until dissolved. Mix in the cold kombucha. Pour into an 8-inch mold and chill in the refrigerator until set, 2 to 4 hours, depending on depth of mold.

To serve, dip the mold in hot water to loosen, invert onto a serving plate, and serve.

AGAR-AGAR VARIATION

In a saucepan, heat 2 cups plain kombucha until you start to see steam rising from the pan. Add 1 tablespoon agar-agar flakes (or 1½ teaspoons agar-agar powder) and 2 tablespoons evaporated cane sugar. Stir well and bring to a boil. Decrease the heat and simmer, stirring often so the sugar doesn't stick to the bottom, until both the agar-agar and sugar have dissolved, about 5 minutes. Pour the mixture into an 8-inch mold and proceed with the recipe.

STRAWBERRY CITRUS BASIL SORBET

If you don't have an ice cream maker, here's a sorbet recipe that still works (if you have a blender or food processor). I like to make this with Meyer lemons, but the combination of kombucha and citrus can get a bit tart, so feel free to experiment with limes or navel oranges until you find a flavor you like. The Grand Marnier is just to help keep the sorbet from freezing all the way—actually, any type of alcohol would work. SERVES 2

1³/₄ cups plain kombucha (page 19)

8 cups strawberries, hulled

¹/₂ to ³/₄ cup citrus juice, plus more as needed

2 tablespoons honey, plus more as needed

2 tablespoons Grand Marnier

2 tablespoons chopped fresh basil

Combine the kombucha, strawberries, citrus juice, honey, and Grand Marnier in a blender or food processor and puree until smooth. Adjust the honey and citrus to taste. Pour into a 1-gallon freezer bag and freeze. When semi-solid, remove and break into pieces. Use a blender or food processor to puree the pieces. Stir in the chopped basil. Serve or store in the freezer for up to 2 weeks.

KOMBUCHA PEAR SORBET

Some people enjoy sorbet as a palate cleanser between courses, but I like to save it for the end of my meal. Sorbets are a little lighter than most ice creams and usually feature some type of fruit. By using kombucha, you cut down on the amount of simple syrup, but not on the fruity flavor. The texture stays the same, too—smooth, soft, and velvety. Add some candied ginger or scatter some chopped-up pear on top to finish your meal with a flourish.

SERVES 2 TO 4

2 cups pear puree (from about 4 pears, peeled and cored)

3 tablespoons ginger puree (from about a 4-inch knob peeled fresh ginger)

14 tablespoons simple syrup (page 73)

1 1/4 cups plain kombucha (page 19)

Combine the pear puree, ginger puree, simple syrup, and kombucha in a bowl and mix until smooth. Add the mix to an ice cream maker and churn according to the manufacturer's instructions. The mix will be soft after churning; place in a freezer for at least 20 minutes to firm up. Serve and enjoy!

KOMBUCHA MELON SORBET

If you're looking for a way to brighten your day—or at least your meal—consider this brilliant melon sorbet featuring honeydew, lime, and midori, a melon liqueur. Midori means "green" in Japanese, so you're basically making a green, green, green sorbet with this recipe. Keeping with the "green" theme, you could save electricity by using a hand-cranked ice cream maker, but if you've already had your workout for the day, an electric ice cream maker will also work. Either way, your friends will be green with envy when they taste your kombucha melon sorbet. SERVES 2 TO 4

3 cups honeydew melon puree (from $^1/_4$ to $^1/_2$ melon, seeded and scooped)

$1^1/_4$ cups plain kombucha (page 19)

$^3/_4$ cup simple syrup (page 73)

2 tablespoons lime zest, finely grated

1 tablespoon freshly squeezed lime juice

2 tablespoons Midori

In a bowl, mix together the melon puree, kombucha, simple syrup, lime zest, lime juice, and Midori until well blended. Pour the mixture into an ice cream maker and churn according to the manufacturer's instructions. The mix will be soft after churning; place in a freezer for 3 to 4 hours to firm up. Serve and enjoy.

OH-SO-NICE FLOAT

When you're craving something sweet with a healthy twist, try this old-fashioned ice cream float with a new-fashioned flavor. The honey and kombucha meld together, bringing a sweet-sour overtone to your ice cream of choice. Don't wait until the end of the day to enjoy this treat; take a few minutes in the early afternoon to prepare this simple but oh-so-nice pick-me-up. Don't forget the swirl—it's your signature on your unique ice cream creation. SERVES 1

2 scoops ice cream
(any flavor)

2 tablespoons honey

$^1/_2$ cup plain kombucha
(page 19)

Fill an ice cream float glass with your favorite ice cream. Mix the honey into the kombucha. Swirl over the top and enjoy!

PRUNE, KOMBUCHA, AND AÑEJO TEQUILA ICE CREAM

Chef Cathy Whims of Portland's Nostrana has taken kombucha to the next level. This indulgent gelato was inspired by an ice cream made with prune and Armagnac, a French brandy similar to Cognac. Here, substitute añejo tequila for the Armagnac and kombucha for the tea traditionally used to soak the prunes. You're going to need some extra time for this one (4 to 5 days to soak the prunes), but it will be worth the wait. Delicious with a sprinkle of spicy chile powder (such as ancho) on top. MAKES 1 QUART

1 cup pitted prunes

2 cups plain kombucha (page 19)

1/4 cup añejo tequila

2 cups heavy cream

2 cups whole milk

3/4 cup evaporated cane sugar

Pinch of sea salt

8 egg yolks

Cover the prunes with the kombucha and soak in the refrigerator for at least 4 days and up to a week.

Drain the prunes, discard the kombucha, and soak at least overnight with the tequila.

Combine the cream and milk in a saucepan with the sugar and salt and heat over medium heat, stirring often, until scalded (just below boiling, when the mixture starts to steam). Remove from heat. Beat the egg yolks in a bowl. Slowly whisk the cream mixture into the egg yolks.

Pour the mixture into the saucepan and cook, stirring over medium-low heat, until the custard forms and the mixture coats a spoon (this can take up to 10 minutes). Strain the mixture immediately through a sieve into a clean bowl. Refrigerate until chilled, about 30 minutes.

Drain the prunes (if necessary) and coarsely chop. Pour the chilled custard into an ice cream maker and start churning according to the manufacturer's directions. When the custard is three-quarters of the way to being frozen, fold in the prunes. Finish freezing and remove from ice cream maker. Serve, or store in the freezer for up to 2 weeks.

MANGO BOOZE-ICE

First there was the snowball, then the snow cone, and eventually shave ice out of Hawaii—all frozen water treats served with a splash of fruity syrup. Now introducing the one and only booze-cone, an alcoholic version of the kiddie ice treats that came before it. Kombucha is an excellent base for this chunky, fruity, boozy treat. Serve this adults-only icy mixture in martini or milk-shake glasses as a play on the plastic cone-shaped cups of yesteryear.

SERVES 4

1 ripe mango

2 cups plain kombucha (page 19)

$^1/_4$ cup freshly squeezed lemon juice

$^1/_2$ cup apple juice

2 tablespoons evaporated cane sugar

2 tablespoons (1 ounce) vodka

To make the mango puree, peel the mango, slice the flesh, and remove the pit. Process the flesh in a blender or food processor until soft. Measure out 1 cup.

Combine the mango puree, kombucha, lemon juice, apple juice, sugar, and vodka in mixing bowl. Mix until the sugar is dissolved.

Transfer the mixture to a shallow baking dish (glass is preferable) and freeze. Every 15 to 20 minutes, break up the mixture with a fork until the liquid is frozen and the mixture has a texture similar to a snow cone. Scoop into glasses and serve.

ABOUT THE AUTHORS

STEPHEN LEE has a rich forty-year history with tea. From Stash Tea, which he and his partners established in 1972, to Tea Tibet, which launched in 2013, Stephen has been at the forefront of the tea business in America. He and his partners launched their best-known brand, Tazo Tea, in 1993 and later sold it to Starbucks. It was on one of his many trips to Russia while running Teaports, an international tea-exporting business, that Stephen discovered kombucha. He founded Kombucha Wonder Drink in 2001. It can now be found in natural foods stores, grocery stores, pubs, spas, college campuses, and coffee and tea houses in all fifty US states, plus Canada, New Zealand, Australia, Malaysia, Belgium, Spain, France, and several Scandinavian countries. Stephen lives with his wife in Portland, Oregon. Visit www.wonderdrink.com.

KEN KOOPMAN, cofounder of the marketing communications agency Koopman Ostbo (www.koopmanostbo .com), has represented brands such as Kettle Chips, Pacific Foods, Yoshida's Fine Sauces, and Bob's Red Mill Natural Foods. He is the author of *People Before Profit: The Inspiring Story of the Founder of Bob's Red Mill*. Ken lives with his wife in Portland, Oregon.

CREDITS

The kombucha community is a creative bunch of brewers and culinary professionals who are making and using kombucha in revolutionary ways. Their inspiration helped me make this book a richer and more varied resource than it would have been otherwise.

Mary Admasian, Aqua Vitea Kombucha
Bristol, Vermont
aquavitea.com
Lemonade Berry Blast Smoothie,
Citrus Sunshine Martini, Edamame
Kombucha Spread, Citrus Salad
Dressing, Kombucha Lime Ceviche

Rich Awn, Founder, Mombucha
Brooklyn, New York
mombucha.wordpress.com
Black Jack Kombucha, Ginger Rail
Kombucha, Blue Eyes

Maya Carlile, Oregon Culinary Institute
Portland, Oregon
www.oregonculinaryinstitute.com
Strawberry Citrus Basil Sorbet

Kyle Christy, Oregon Culinary Institute
Portland, Oregon
www.oregonculinaryinstitute.com
Kombucha Root Beer Sasparilla,
Old West

Dustin Clark, Executive Chef,
Wildwood Restaurant
Portland, Oregon
wildwoodrestaurant.com
Kombucha Tea-Brined Eggs, Kombucha
Ramen Noodles

Hannah Crum, "Kombucha Mamma,"
Kombucha Kamp
Beverly Hills, California
www.kombuchakamp.com
Blood Orange Italian Soda

Jeff Delkin, Owner, Bambu
Portland, Oregon
www.bambuhome.com
BambuCha

Scott Dolich, Chef-Owner,
Park Kitchen and The Bent Brick
Portland, Oregon
parkkitchen.com, thebentbrick.com
Kombucha Mignonette

Beth Eakin, Oregon Culinary Institute
Portland, Oregon
www.oregonculinaryinstitute.com
Kombucha Five Spice Syrup

William Elder, Co-Owner, Valentine's
Portland, Oregon
www.valentinespdx.com
Seanz Kafka

Susan Fink, Owner, Karma Kombucha
Vernon Hills, Illinois
karmaboocha.com
Pomegranate-Cranberry Combo,
Pasta Salad with Kombucha Herb Dressing

Rachel Kanaan, Cofounder,
Unity Vibration Kombucha
Ypsilanti, Michigan
http://unityvibrationkombucha.com
Green Smoothie

Jovial King, Founder, and Leah Eide,
Urban Moonshine
Burlington, Vermont
www.urbanmoonshine.com
Moonshine Cocktail

Beth Koroleski
Portland, Oregon
Alaskan Cod Fish Tacos, Kombucha
Coleslaw

Eileen Laird, Founder,
Phoenix Helix
www.phoenixhelix.com
Holiday Spice Kombucha, Lavender
Lemonade Kombucha

Oona J. Meade, Komboona Skincare
Ashland, Oregon
Boochie Salt Scrub

Geoff Millner, Oregon Culinary
Institute
Portland, Oregon
www.oregonculinaryinstitute.com
Long Kombucha Iced Tea, Gingered
Pearbucha, Kombucha Dipping Sauce,
Kombucha Mushrooms, Kombucha
Tropical Fruit Salad, Kombucha Pear
Sorbet, Kombucha Melon Sorbet

Sharon Moliken, Earthwise Gourmet
Portland, Oregon
www.earthwisegourmet.com
Baby's Paw, Over the Rainbow

Warren Moliken, Wabi O Kombucha
Christchurch, New Zealand
www.wabio.co.nz
Able & Baker's Blastoff Fruition
Smoothie

Rosalyn Newhouse, Cultures for Health
www.culturesforhealth.com
Kombucha Mustard

Jonathan Ojinaga and Edgar Tamayo,
Owners, Azúcar Lounge
San Francisco, California
www.azucarsf.com
Yerba Buena

Princeton and Jennifer R.
Kennebunkport, Maine
Kombucha Vegan Chèvre Spread

Linda Dalal Sawaya, Author,
Alice's Kitchen: Traditional Lebanese Cooking
lindasawaya.com
Mangobucha Tropical Dressing

David Shenaut, Bar Manager,
Raven and Rose
Portland, Oregon
www.ravenandrosepdx.com
Impossible Dream

Meghan Telpner, Tonica Kombucha
Toronto, Ontario
www.tonicakombucha.com
Blueberry Mojito Mocktail

Justin Trout, Cofounder,
Health-Ade Kombucha
Los Angeles, California
health-ade.com
*Seasonal Sangria, International Elder,
Healthy Mule, Smooth Recovery, Harvest
Breakfast Bread with Kombucha
Sourdough Starter, Oh-So-Nice Float*

Ryan Victor, Bar Manager, Tapalaya
Portland, Oregon
www.tapalaya.com
Sweet Italian, Cranberry Bitters Cocktail

Cathy Whims, Executive Chef,
Nostrana
Portland, Oregon
nostrana.com
*Prune, Kombucha, and Añejo Tequila
Ice Cream*

Justin Wiese, Chef,
Multnomah Athletic Club
Portland, Oregon
www.themac.com
*Kombucha Ginger Marinade, Green Papaya
Salad, Mango Booze-Ice*

Chrissie Manion Zaerpoor, Owner,
Kookoolan Farms and
Kookoolan World Meadery
Yamhill, Oregon
www.kookoolanfarms.com
*Kombucha Vinegar, Wilted Spinach
with Bacon-Kombucha Dressing,
Kombucha Sunomono*

MEASUREMENT CONVERSION CHART

VOLUME

US	IMPERIAL	METRIC
1 tablespoon	$^1/_2$ fl oz	15 ml
2 tablespoons	1 fl oz	30 ml
$^1/_4$ cup	2 fl oz	60 ml
$^1/_3$ cup	3 fl oz	90 ml
$^1/_2$ cup	4 fl oz	120 ml
$^2/_3$ cup	5 fl oz ($^1/_4$ pint)	150 ml
$^3/_4$ cup	6 fl oz	180 ml
1 cup	8 fl oz ($^1/_3$ pint)	240 ml
$1^1/_4$ cups	10 fl oz ($^1/_2$ pint)	300 ml
2 cups (1 pint)	16 fl oz ($^2/_3$ pint)	480 ml
$2^1/_2$ cups	20 fl oz (1 pint)	600 ml
1 quart	32 fl oz ($1^2/_3$ pints)	1 l

TEMPERATURE

FAHRENHEIT	CELSIUS/GAS MARK
250°F	120°C/gas mark $^1/_2$
275°F	135°C/gas mark 1
300°F	150°C/gas mark 2
325°F	160°C/gas mark 3
350°F	180 or 175°C/gas mark 4
375°F	190°C/gas mark 5
400°F	200°C/gas mark 6
425°F	220°C/gas mark 7
450°F	230°C/gas mark 8
475°F	245°C/gas mark 9
500°F	260°C

LENGTH

INCH	METRIC
$^1/_4$ inch	6 mm
$^1/_2$ inch	1.25 cm
$^3/_4$ inch	2 cm
1 inch	2.5 cm
6 inches ($^1/_2$ foot)	15 cm
12 inches (1 foot)	30 cm

WEIGHT

US/IMPERIAL	METRIC
$^1/_2$ oz	15 g
1 oz	30 g
2 oz	60 g
$^1/_4$ lb	115 g
$^1/_3$ lb	150 g
$^1/_2$ lb	225 g
$^3/_4$ lb	350 g
1 lb	450 g

INDEX

Published in the United States by Ten Speed Press, an imprint of the Crown Publishing Group, a division of Random House LLC, a Penguin Random House Company, New York.
www.crownpublishing.com
www.tenspeed.com

Author photographs appearing in the introduction and author page copyright © 2013 by Todd Eckelman Photography

Library of Congress Cataloging-in-Publication Data
Lee, Stephen, 1943-
  Kombucha revolution : 75 recipes for homemade brews, fixers, elixirs, and mixers / Stephen Lee with Ken Koopman ; photography by Leo Gong. —First edition.
     pages cm
  Includes index.
1. Kombucha tea. I. Koopman, Ken. II. Title.
  TX817.T3L44 2014
  641.87'7—dc23
                                2013040309

Hardcover ISBN: 978-1-60774-598-3
eBook ISBN: 978-1-60774-599-0

Printed in China

Design by Chloe Rawlins
Interior food styling by Karen Shinto
Interior prop styling by Carol Hacker

10 9 8 7 6 5

First Edition